2 TIMOTHY & TITUS

A 40-DAY BIBLE STUDY

"This daily devotional is something I've longed for. It is expositional, theological, and practical as it walks verse by verse through a book of the Bible in just 40 days. With such an outstanding stable of contributors, it is certain to become widely used in the days to come."

DANIEL L. AKIN,
president, Southeastern Baptist Theological Seminary,
North Carolina

"I cannot think of a greater gift to the church than a biblically rooted devotional series, which spans the entire New Testament. Christians need to study the Bible, and they need to read it devotionally, prayerfully, and expecting God's power to manifest through their reading of the pages of Scripture. The Planted in the Word series—which works through the Bible book by book, chapter by chapter, and line by line—will nourish the faith of Christians in a profound way for many years to come."

R. ALBERT MOHLER,
president, The Southern Baptist Theological Seminary,
Kentucky

"Let's be honest: daily Bible reading and prayer can get stale and tiresome. We need a fresh angle! The Planted in the Word volumes provide it. Seasoned scholars explain the text, relate it to Christ, apply it, and offer a sample prayer. Additional questions facilitate personal growth or group discussion. This is a treasure chest of Bible exposition, not random but rather in the flow of each biblical book. Follow these guides for a clearer grasp of Scripture, direction in living it out, and motivation for rich, Scripture-grounded communion with God."

ROBERT W. YARBROUGH,
professor of New Testament, Covenant Theological Seminary,
Missouri

"As a pastor, I'm constantly seeking resources that help our congregation dive deeper into the Scriptures—reading, understanding, and living out God's Word. The Planted in the Word series delivers this in an outstanding way. The level of scholarship throughout is truly exceptional, and I have great trust and respect for each of the contributors. I'm excited to place these valuable tools in the hands of our church members, knowing they will be well-equipped to grow in their faith."

JASON DEES,
senior pastor, Christ Covenant,
Atlanta, Georgia

2 TIMOTHY & TITUS

A 40-DAY BIBLE STUDY

SAM STORMS

Benjamin L. Merkle, Series Editor

LEXHAM PRESS

2 Timothy and Titus: A 40-Day Bible Study
Planted in the Word, edited by Benjamin L. Merkle

Lexham Press, 1313 Commercial St., Bellingham, WA 98225
LexhamPress.com

Print ISBN 9781683597865
Digital ISBN 9781683597872
Library of Congress Control Number 2024946239

Lexham Editorial: Elliot Ritzema, Allisyn Ma, Danielle Burlaga, Mandi Newell
Cover Design: Joshua Hunt
Typesetting: Justin Marr

24 25 26 27 28 29 30 / US / 12 11 10 9 8 7 6 5 4 3 2 1

Joyfully dedicated to the men of the Theological Roundtable,
with special gratitude to our leader,
Dudley Hall

Contents

Series Preface

The longest book of the Bible begins by describing someone who is blessed (Ps 1:1–3). Such a person does not walk with the wicked, stand with sinners, or sit with scoffers. Instead, they delight in God's law, meditating on it day and night. They are further described as a tree that is located in an ideal setting—it is planted by streams of water. Water brings nourishment and sustenance to a tree. Without water, a tree will wither and die. But with sufficient water comes growth, causing the tree to produce its fruit. Where the tree is planted makes all the difference. If it is planted by a stream, it has a continual source of life-giving water.

God's word is the water that nourishes the soul. Without it, we spiritually wither or shrivel, and in order to continue "life as normal" we are forced to draw sustenance from other places—places that were never designed to give us what only God can. The goal of this series is to help you experience God's blessing by planting you beside the stream of God's life-giving word. Each volume consists of forty days of guided Bible study through a particular book (or books) of the New Testament. And each day's study consists of five components:

1. *Read* the passage of Scripture.
2. *Meditate* on the meaning of the text.

3. *Reflect on Christ*, since all the promises of God are "yes" and "amen" in him (2 Cor 1:20).

4. *Apply God's Word* because it is alive and active, and is what God uses to transform us into the image of his Son.

5. *Pray*, asking for God's help.

Additionally, the *Study It Further* section provides a way for you to dig deeper by examining how the Old Testament provides the background for the passage, by looking at a particular word or theme elsewhere in the New Testament, or by encouraging you to consider how the passage relates to you personally.

So, drink deeply from God's word. Let us not be like those who are influenced by the things of this world, causing us to drift further and further away from God (from walking, to standing, and eventually to sitting with the wicked). Instead, let us be planted in the word, drawing continual nourishment for our souls through the life-giving and fruit-producing words of the living God.

Benjamin L. Merkle
Series Editor

Introduction to 2 Timothy and Titus

The apostle Paul likely met Timothy for the first time during the course of his second missionary journey. Although Timothy was certainly well-versed in the Hebrew Scriptures (2 Tim 3:15), it may well have been Paul who led him to saving faith in Jesus (see 1 Cor 4:15–17; 1 Tim 1:2). Although we don't know how Titus came to faith in Christ, he was clearly a member of Paul's inner circle of highly trusted friends and traveling companions. A compelling case can be made that Titus accompanied Paul on a missionary journey to Crete (Titus 1:5), most likely after the events of Acts 28 and before the composition of 2 Timothy. The two of them established a church on the island, after which Paul departed, leaving Titus there to oversee its early growth. A lawyer named Zenas, together with another brother, Apollos (Titus 3:13), are thought to have carried the letter to Titus in Crete.

Paul's second letter to Timothy, and his short letter to Titus, have exerted a tremendous influence on the life of all Christians, elders, pastors, and other church leaders in particular. Whereas Paul most likely wrote Titus (as well as 1 Timothy) after his release from his first Roman imprisonment (the approximate date of which would be no later than AD 62), 2 Timothy was written during Paul's second Roman imprisonment. He is incarcerated in the belly of a Roman prison, perhaps only weeks away from being beheaded on the order of Nero, emperor of Rome. There is a sense, then, that what we have in this short epistle is Paul's last will and testament. It is his concluding exhortation not only to Timothy but to the entire church of Jesus Christ. Although we can't be certain, Luke may have served as Paul's amanuensis, or scribe, in the composition of this letter.

While some may think it more appropriate to study 1 and 2 Timothy together, rather than 2 Timothy and Titus, the latter pairing is more plausible if for no other reason than that they are Paul's final two letters. There is a sense of urgency in Titus and 2 Timothy, especially relating to the threat of false teachers, persecution, and the need for endurance. Titus was likely written in the waning months of Paul's life and 2 Timothy perhaps only weeks prior to his execution. They both serve as Paul's final and thus most mature reflections on the gospel and the need to guard its purity. There is also the special, spiritual relationship that both men sustained with Paul. Timothy is his "beloved child" (2 Tim 1:2) and Titus his "true child in a common faith" (Titus 1:4).

The downside to identifying an overall theme of 2 Timothy and Titus is the tendency to ignore the details of the many particular issues facing both men in their ministries. Still, though, we can easily see in these two epistles Paul's pressing concern for the godly character of both men and the threat from false teachers who were seemingly indifferent to God's standards of behavior. The repeated appeals to guard the gospel and be alert to those "who turn away from the truth" (Titus 1:14) is only one reason why studying the two together is spiritually beneficial.

AUTHORSHIP

Some scholars have questioned Paul's authorship of both 2 Timothy and Titus, contending that they are examples of pseudepigraphy in which an anonymous individual or group of individuals composed both letters well after Paul's death and circulated them under Paul's name, as if he were the author. However, the evidence supporting Paul having written all of the so-called Pastoral Epistles (1–2 Timothy and Titus) is quite strong and need not detain us here. In any case, most agree that 2 Timothy is undeniably from Paul. What we can know with a high degree of confidence is that Paul's second Roman imprisonment (the first is described in Acts 28) would have fallen within the range of AD 64–68, the period during which Nero launched his persecution of Christians in the city. Most believe Paul was executed in AD 67 (although some place the date as early as AD 64). Tradition suggests that he was beheaded at Aquae Salviae near the third milestone on what is known as the Ostian Way.

PRIMARY THEME

As the studies below will show, the primary theme of 2 Timothy is Paul's appeal to his young protégé to endure suffering for the gospel without shame or fear. Paul undoubtedly felt the shadow of the executioner's sword hovering above his head and thus speaks urgently and passionately about the importance of Christ's servants remaining faithful to the gospel in the face of all manner of opposition.

The short letter from Paul to Titus contains instructions on how he was to put local church matters in order on the island of Crete (Titus 1:5). We can't be sure where Paul was when he wrote it, and he may have composed it even in the midst of his missionary journey, most likely no later than AD 62. By the time Titus received the letter, Paul would have arrived in Nicopolis (Titus 3:12), a port city on the western coast of central Greece.

APOSTLES OR FOLLOWERS?

There is considerable debate as to whether Timothy and Titus were apostles. Paul's first letter to the Thessalonians came from "Paul, Silvanus [Silas], and Timothy" (1 Thess 1:1). Later, in chapter 2, Paul appears to include those two men with him in the company of apostles: "Nor did we seek glory from people, whether from you or from others, though we could have made demands as apostles of Christ" (1 Thess 2:6). The primary reason for excluding Timothy is the belief that to be an apostle one had to have been an eyewitness to the risen Christ. But if the latter qualification only applied to the original twelve and Paul, it would have no bearing on Timothy's call to the apostolate. Titus is also often mentioned as a possible apostle, given his prominent role alongside Paul. Although not explicitly called an apostle, his authority as one who labored with Paul suggests that he, too, was regarded as one (see 2 Cor 2:12–13; 7:6, 13, 14; 8:6, 16, 23; 12:18; Gal 2:1–14; 2 Tim 4:10; Titus 1:5).

Those who question whether Timothy and Titus were apostles typically argue that neither of the two were elders or overseers in their respective churches but served as apostolic legates or temporary delegates commissioned by Paul to set matters in place. Of course, this is an argument from silence. Nothing explicitly in either 2 Timothy or Titus precludes the possibility that they served in a local pastoral capacity.

2 Timothy

Day 1

2 Timothy 1:1–2

READ

Paul, an apostle of Christ Jesus by the will of God according to the promise of the life that is in Christ Jesus, To Timothy, my beloved child: Grace, mercy, and peace from God the Father and Christ Jesus our Lord.

MEDITATE

To what or to whom do you attribute who you are and what you seek to achieve in life? When times are tough and it feels as if the world is aligned against you, what is the anchor that keeps your soul firmly grounded? It is a profoundly important question, one that the apostle Paul never failed to answer explicitly. I am an apostle, says Paul, but be it known that I did not seek this office or achieve it by means of personal effort or talent or skill. I am an apostle "by the will of God" (for similar language, see Rom 1:1; 1 Cor 1:1; Gal 1:1; Eph 1:1; Col 1:1; 1 Tim 1:1). Writing this epistle from a Roman prison cell, with the shadow of impending death hanging over his head, Paul found strength to persevere in the assurance that it was God's will that had placed him there.

His calling, no less so yours and mine, was "according to the promise of the life that is in Christ Jesus" (1:1). This is a healthy reminder that prepositions are important. "According to" (*kata*) normally means in conformity with or in accordance with something. Some have suggested that here it means in consequence of, in the sense that the promise of life in Christ served as the foundation of Paul's apostolic calling. But I believe "according to" more likely directs our attention to the purpose of Paul's apostleship. That is to say, he is an apostle of Christ Jesus for the purpose of proclaiming the promise of eternal life that can only be found in a personal relationship by faith with Jesus Christ. This is confirmed a few verses later when Paul describes himself as having been "appointed a preacher and apostle and teacher" (1:11) to make known the "life and immortality" that comes through the gospel (1:10).

Together with this promise of life comes "grace, mercy, and peace" (1:2b). We see from this and numerous other texts that God's "grace" is more than a principle in accordance with which God has forgiven us of our sins. It is also a power, the very presence of the Holy Spirit sustaining and encouraging us in our daily battle with the world, the flesh, and the devil. So, too, God's mercy and peace are experiential blessings by which God keeps us faithful and strong in whatever adverse circumstances we face. We must never forget that Paul is perhaps no more than days, at most weeks, from suffering execution as a martyr for Christ. He himself would find power to persevere from the grace, mercy, and peace that flows from the heart of God into the heart of each of his children. And, as is typical in Paul's letters, while he opens with a promise that such blessings will come from God to us, he concludes with the prayer that such will be *with* us as we press on in life (4:22).

REFLECT ON CHRIST

We live in a day when insisting on the exclusivity of Jesus Christ as the only path to reconciliation with God is ridiculed as arrogant and elitist. Paul, needless to say, would disagree. The promise of eternal life is found in Christ Jesus and in Christ Jesus alone. This is an echo of what is consistently taught elsewhere in the New Testament (see John 14:6; Acts 4:12; 1 John 2:23). That God should provide for hell-deserving sinners even so much as a single path to forgiveness and salvation is itself a marvelous and immeasurable expression of undeserved mercy.

We should note that what makes this declaration so reassuring is that this "life" is a promise from God. A promise, of course, is only as good and certain as the character of the one who makes it. And it is God himself who promises life to all who by faith embrace Jesus Christ and the sufficiency of his life, death, and resurrection. Scripture doesn't say that he who has the Son *may* obtain life, but in the words of John the apostle, "whoever has the Son *has* life" (1 John 5:12).[1]

APPLY GOD'S WORD

Paul's reference to the will of God does not mean that he was coerced against his own will to embrace this calling, but God's will ultimately accounts for Paul's authority and the power with which he discharged this ministry. Such is true of each of us, though few, if any of us, I suspect, would lay claim to being an apostle. If you are a faithful wife to your husband and devoted to your children, it is only by God's will that such is true. If you are a student in seminary, having sensed a call into pastoral ministry, it is only by God's will that such is true. If you feel the prompting in your heart to take the gospel to an unreached

1. Emphases in Scripture are added by the author.

people group and are willing to forego the comforts of life in Western culture, it is only by God's will that such is true. God has orchestrated life in this way to ensure that he alone receives the glory for whatever we achieve in our various endeavors. It matters little if you are a teacher, a pastor, a housewife, a student, or a construction worker—your labor must always be undertaken with the conscious awareness of having been called by the will of God.

PRAY

Gracious, merciful Heavenly Father, I confess that all the good I have, especially the promise of eternal life in Christ Jesus, is due solely to your kind and benevolent will. Simple words of gratitude seem so inadequate, so disproportionate to such a marvelous blessing that you have bestowed, but I say thank you, nonetheless, to the glory and praise of your great name. Amen.

STUDY IT FURTHER

1. How do we reconcile God's will for our lives with our personal desires and goals? To which should we give priority?

2. Read Hebrews 6:13–20. When God makes a promise to us, is it always guaranteed to come to pass? How does this passage in Hebrews address that question?

3. Grace, mercy, and peace come to us not only from God the Father but also from Christ Jesus. What does this tell us about the relationship between the Father and the Son? Read Romans 16:27; 1 Corinthians 1:3.

PRAY

I thank you, great Triune God, Father, Son, and Holy Spirit, that in your all-sufficiency you graciously supply me with all I need. May I never come to you or pretend to serve you as if you were in need of me. It is I who am in desperate, daily, moment-by-moment need of you. Amen.

STUDY IT FURTHER

1. What is the "conscience"? What role does it play in Christian experience and decision-making? Which is more authoritative: our conscience or the written word of God?

2. Why did Paul think it important to align himself with his "ancestors"? Whom does he have in mind and why is this important?

3. Read Philippians 1:3–4. Why did Paul place such a profound emphasis on constancy in prayer? Are there people in your life for whom you are always in prayer?

Day 3

2 Timothy 1:4–5

READ

As I remember your tears, I long to see you, that I may be filled with joy. I am reminded of your sincere faith, a faith that dwelt first in your grandmother Lois and your mother Eunice and now, I am sure, dwells in you as well.

MEDITATE

Earlier in verse 2 Paul referred to Timothy as his "beloved child." Paul had no biological children, but Timothy was as dear and precious to him as any natural son or daughter possibly could be. Paul himself spoke of his "spiritual mother" in Romans 16:13, so it comes as no surprise that he envisioned his relationship with Timothy along familial lines.

Paul does not identify the occasion or cause for Timothy's tears, but he likely has in mind the time of separation that occurred because of his arrest and subsequent imprisonment. The picture of Timothy's sorrow as Paul was being dragged off to Rome stimulated the apostle's desire to be reunited with his spiritual son and experience the joy that this sort of relationship evokes in the human heart.

The more accurate translation of the opening words of verse 4 is "having received a reminder" of your tears, a reference perhaps to the receipt of a letter or some news about Timothy's condition. We know from Acts 16:1–3 that Timothy's father was not a Christian. But the young boy was not for this reason at a disadvantage, as both his grandmother and mother were present to train him in the truth of the Scriptures (see 2 Tim 3:14–15). The faith that dwelt in these ladies was certainly that of two devout Israelites who anticipated the coming Messiah. But it was also faith in Jesus Christ as this promised one, given the fact that Paul is confident the same kind of faith now dwells in Timothy.

There is much to learn from Paul's regular practice of praying for his friends and those converted to Christ through his ministry. What we read here of his prayers for Timothy was not an isolated or rare activity. He prayed for both the Romans (Rom 1:9) and the Christians in Colossae (Col 1:3), in spite of the fact that he had never visited either city and only knew of believers there from having made their acquaintance during prior travels. And, lest we forget, the absence of physical comforts should never factor in to whether or for how long we pray for those with whom God has united us. Paul was alone, in a Roman dungeon, but his intercessory petitions were not for that reason any less frequent or fervent.

Paul was just as committed to requesting prayers for himself as he was in praying for those whom he loved. He concludes his letter to the Romans by appealing to them "to strive together" in their "prayers to God" on his behalf (Rom 15:30). Whether they are prayers by an apostle for an average believer, or by you and me on behalf of our spiritual leaders, God has called us to partner with him in the implementation of his will on the earth. We dare not neglect so great a privilege and so effective a power.

REFLECT ON CHRIST

When Paul prayed for Timothy, or Timothy for Paul, the standard verbiage was to ask the Father, in the name of the Son, and in the power of the Holy Spirit. But this is more than mere verbiage; it is profoundly theological and reflects the biblical emphasis on the role of the Trinity in the prayer lives of God's people.

Jesus assured his followers that "if you ask me anything in my name, I will do it" (John 14:14). Praying "in the name" of Jesus is far more than simply tacking those words onto the back end of our petitions. We must never think that there is some magical power in specific words. The power of prayer is related to the person whose name we utter. To ask "in Jesus's name" is to do so with a conscious dependence on his sinless life, substitutionary death, and bodily resurrection as the sole grounds on which we can approach the Father. It is to pray with one supreme desire, that the name of Jesus be extolled and adored and that his will be done. And when this praying is done in the power of the Holy Spirit (Rom 8:26–27; Eph 6:18; Jude 20), we can rest assured that our petitions are heard and whatever grace and mercy we need will be supplied (Heb 4:16).

APPLY GOD'S WORD

There is something precious about the relationship that Paul had with his spiritual son, Timothy. Can we say the same thing about ourselves and those with whom God has united us in the life of the local church? In a day when people have withdrawn from the corporate life of the body of Christ, thinking to themselves that they stand in need of no one, we must cultivate a hunger for the blessings of fellowship and intimacy that can only be found in the mutual encouragement and prayer support of believers.

We will later on take note of Paul's solemn lament that, as he remained imprisoned in Rome, "Luke alone is with me" (2 Tim 4:11). Paul felt the urgent need for the physical presence and the spiritual encouragement that can come only from other brothers and sisters in Christ. We are not an island unto ourselves, and it will only work to our spiritual disadvantage should we fail to seek out others and profit from their faith and commitment to Christ.

If you are currently unattached to a local church, cut off from the spiritual blessings and power that God wills to be communicated from one Christian to another, Paul would urge you to seek out a body of believers where you can flourish to the praise and glory of Jesus.

PRAY

Father, I come to you in the name of your Son and my Savior, Jesus, because of who he is and what he has done, and in the sustaining and motivating power of the Holy Spirit, and I ask that you embed me in a community of faith where I can grow in mutual encouragement and accountability (Rom 1:11–12). Amen.

STUDY IT FURTHER

1. Paul's "joy" was to some extent dependent on his relationship with Timothy. Are there people in your life whose presence and influence contributes to your joy? If so, might you express this to them in much the same way that Paul did to Timothy?

2. Are there extended family members in your life who have contributed to the growth of your faith? Reflect on their influence. Do you regularly give thanks for them?

3. Paul seems quite confident that Timothy's faith is "sincere." On what does he base this? Read John 8:31 and explore how the words of Jesus would assist Paul in his assessment of Timothy.

Day 4

2 Timothy 1:6–7

READ

For this reason I remind you to fan into flame the gift of God, which is in you through the laying on of my hands, for God gave us a spirit not of fear but of power and love and self-control.

MEDITATE

The "reason" (v. 6a) to which Paul refers is likely a reference back to Timothy's sincere faith in verse 5. It is because he knows full well the quality and intensity of Timothy's faith that he does not hesitate to exhort him to rekindle the gift that God has bestowed on him.

The verb translated "fan into flame" may mean no more than to "stir up" or keep alive the fire that was already burning. The verb is present tense, suggesting that Timothy should persist in sustaining the work of the Spirit in him. But the likelihood is that Timothy, for some reason, had become lax and even a bit irresponsible in the exercise of this gift. Paul's exhortation would thus be to rekindle the fire of the Spirit's presence in his life. It is possible for us to neglect a spiritual gift and fail to put it to the use for which God designed it. Paul likely envisions Timothy's gift as a barely burning ember that needs to be blown upon and stoked back into full flame.

The precise identity or nature of this "gift" (*charisma*) is not specified, but there are numerous possibilities. He may be referring to the ministry itself to which Timothy had been called. Others suggest it was the gift of evangelism (see 2 Tim 4:5), or perhaps administration, or even some special empowering work of the Spirit that Paul deemed essential for his labors.

Whatever the nature of this *charisma,* it was imparted to Timothy "through the laying on" of Paul's "hands" (v. 6b). There is no indication that this is the only means by which the Spirit imparts a spiritual gift, but it is surely one of them. In 1 Timothy 4:14, Paul mentions yet another (or the same?) gift that came by prophecy "when the council of elders laid their hands on" Timothy. The Spirit, of course, is always free to distribute spiritual gifts according to his will (1 Cor 12:11).

Timothy should not be in the least hesitant to heed Paul's counsel, because ("for") God did not give him or anyone else (including us) a spirit of fear but of "power and love and self-control" (v. 7). Fear should play no part in a Christian's life or ministry. The Holy Spirit is present and permanently in us in order that we might operate in God's power, which is essential to Timothy if he is to withstand hostility and persecution. Love should always be our ultimate aim, as spiritual gifts are clearly given for the building up of others in the body of Christ. This power operating through us will never be chaotic or uncontrollable.

That the Spirit produces these virtues in us is a reminder that they are not native talents or the fruit of our painstaking effort. If we are to exercise our giftings and fulfill our ministry in a disciplined manner, these must be understood as the gracious endowments of the Holy Spirit.

REFLECT ON CHRIST

Although Jesus is not explicitly mentioned in our text, it is he who is ultimately responsible for the gift of the Holy Spirit. In his instruction to the disciples in the upper room, he made it clear that he would ask the Father to give us "another Helper" to be with us forever (John 14:16). For this reason, I am persuaded that "spirit" in verse 7 should be capitalized. It is the Holy Spirit who has been given to us, who works in and through us by means of certain spiritual gifts (*charismata*). Although it is the Father who sends the Holy Spirit (initially, in his fullness, at Pentecost), he does it, says Jesus, "in my name" (John 14:26).

This is confirmed by Peter in his speech on the day of Pentecost. There he declared that "being exalted at the right hand of God, and having received from the Father the promise of the Holy Spirit, he [Jesus] has poured out this that you yourselves are seeing and hearing" (Acts 2:33). The Spirit, together with his gifts, is in us by virtue of the work of the Son. And he is here primarily to "glorify" Jesus, "for he will take what is mine [a reference to Jesus] and declare it to you" (John 16:14).

APPLY GOD'S WORD

Not every Christian has the same spiritual gifts, but everyone has at least one, as we clearly see in such texts as 1 Corinthians 12:7–10 and Romans 12:6. The apostle Peter could not have been more explicit when he said, "As each has received a gift, use it to serve one another, as good stewards of God's varied grace" (1 Pet 4:10). Here, once again, we see confirmation that spiritual gifts are not the reward for personal merit but are expressions of divine grace.

It may serve you well to pause today and prayerfully examine how you have made use of, or perhaps neglected, whatever gifts the Holy Spirit has imparted to you. Whether you received your gift(s) through the laying on of hands or more directly and immediately by a sovereign act of the Spirit, be diligent to employ them for the glory of Christ and the edification of his people, what Paul refers to as "the common good" (1 Cor 12:7).

And if, for whatever reason, you have neglected to make effective use of your gift, pray that the Spirit would blow on that barely burning ember and bring it back into use for the purpose for which it was given.

PRAY

Father, thank you for reminding me that whatever fear there may be in my life is not from you. Would you awaken in me an ever-increasing awareness of the power, love, and self-control that you have made possible by your Spirit? Please, Father, replace whatever fear remains in my heart with a sense of your abiding love and the stability of your promises to me in Christ. Amen.

STUDY IT FURTHER

1. Read 1 Corinthians 12:7–10. What is the purpose of spiritual gifts? What are your gifts, and how have you made use of them to build up the body of Christ?

2. Are there ways in which you have let the fire of the Spirit's presence in your life diminish? What might you do to rekindle the powerful presence of the Spirit in your life and ministry?

3. Read 1 Timothy 4:14. Why does Paul refer to the laying on of hands and is this a practice that we should follow today?

Day 5

2 Timothy 1:8

READ

Therefore do not be ashamed of the testimony about our Lord, nor of me his prisoner, but share in suffering for the gospel by the power of God ...

MEDITATE

Paul knew well the pressures that come with gospel ministry. He wasn't immune to the temptation to cower in fear and remain silent in the face of ridicule. But he made it clear in his letter to the Romans that he had learned the secret of conquering shame: "For I am not ashamed of the gospel, for it is the power of God for salvation to everyone who believes, to the Jew first and also to the Greek. For in it the righteousness of God is revealed from faith for faith, as it is written, 'The righteous shall live by faith' " (Rom 1:16–17).

This isn't in any way to diminish the power that shame can often exert on the human soul. There are any number of reasons why people might feel ashamed of the gospel. They may live in constant fear of losing face, losing friends, being labeled a fanatic, taunting and scorn, or losing influence. Paul undoubtedly had these same concerns, but he refused to yield to them. Here he calls on his spiritual son to join him in courageously bearing witness to "the testimony about our Lord."

For those who remain steadfast in their gospel proclamation, suffering is inevitable. We must be certain, however, that we suffer not because we sin but because of our unwavering commitment to make known the gospel (v. 8b). If this feels overwhelming and beyond our strength to achieve, Paul is quick to remind Timothy that it comes only by virtue of "the power of God" (v. 8b).

Mention should be made of the relation between verses 6–7 and what follows in verses 8–11, which is indicated by "therefore" in verse 8. Paul had just encouraged Timothy to resist the paralyzing power of fear in gospel ministry (v. 7). In essence he says, "Knowing that the Spirit within you is one of power and love and self-control, avail yourself, Timothy, of what he can do when you are tempted to feel embarrassment on account of Jesus, or perhaps even on account of my current imprisonment."

There are countless ways of avoiding shame. One might rephrase the terms of the gospel, eliminating any offensive elements in it. Or one might be more selective and discerning when it comes to the places and people where the truth is shared. Whatever the allure, says Paul, resist by the power of God all such temptations. The reason is clear. As Paul said in Romans 1:16, the gospel, and only the gospel, has the supernatural capacity to save sinners (see also 1 Cor 1:18; 2:4–5; 4:19–20; 2 Cor 4:7; 6:7; 12:9; Eph 3:7; 1 Thess 1:5). Paul was not ashamed of the gospel because Jesus himself made it plain that there is no other hope for any human being apart from faith in him and his death and resurrection. Paul despised whatever shame he might otherwise have felt because he knew that there is salvation in no one else. Here he appeals to young Timothy to recognize this life-changing truth as well.

REFLECT ON CHRIST

The gospel is "testimony about our Lord," Jesus Christ. Sadly, many today have vastly expanded the gospel to include everything from the restoration of personal self-esteem to environmental care. This is not to say that the gospel does not have wide-ranging implications for life on earth, but we must be diligent to differentiate between the essence of the gospel and its multiple entailments. The content of the gospel must remain pristine and never be confused with its consequences. The gospel is singular in its focus. It is the gloriously good news about what God the Father has done in and through the sinless life, substitutionary death, and bodily resurrection of Jesus Christ to satisfy his justice, assuage his wrath, and reconcile us to himself by securing for us the forgiveness of our sins.

The gospel, therefore, is profoundly and decidedly Christocentric. Where Jesus and his merciful work of living the life we should have lived and couldn't is forgotten, or where Jesus and his gracious offering of himself to die a death that we deserved to die but now never will is diminished, the gospel is not made known.

Paul would never deny that he and Timothy would be *shamed* for preaching the gospel, but that is far different from being *ashamed* of the gospel. We must daily remind ourselves that God's gospel is the only hope for eternal salvation.

APPLY GOD'S WORD

How, then, are we today to heed Paul's counsel never to be ashamed of the gospel concerning Jesus? The only way is by constantly reminding ourselves that in it the saving power of the omnipotent God is released and secures for hell-deserving men and women the forgiveness of sins and deliverance from eternal judgment. The gospel can do what no other religion can accomplish. Not Buddhism, Hinduism, Islam, or any other manmade spiritual solution can confer a righteousness that will avail in the presence of an infinitely holy God.

As wonderful as good physical health is, it will not guarantee eternal life. As uplifting as multiple caring friendships can be, they cannot save us. As helpful as the best education that the best universities in the world can provide is, it will not save us before a righteous God. As encouraging as are the many scientific and technological advances in our world, they are impotent to overcome our moral failures, idolatry, and rebellion against God.

The power resident in the gospel alone can save the lost and give hope to the hopeless, freedom to slaves, guidance to the wandering, purity to the polluted, and purpose to those convinced that life has no value.

PRAY

Father, I am by nature a weak and cowardly person. Infuse me with your power! Grant me your strength that I might courageously stand in the face of all manner of threats and oppositions and faithfully proclaim the good news of Jesus Christ. Amen.

STUDY IT FURTHER

1. Read Ephesians 6:19–20 where Paul asks for prayer that he would speak the truth of the gospel with boldness. If Paul exhorted Timothy not to be ashamed of the gospel, how would he have prayed for his spiritual son? How do you pray for yourself in this regard?

2. Read Romans 8:35–38. How does the promise in this passage empower the believer to embrace suffering for the sake of the gospel? What is the promise that Paul gives to every believer?

3. Paul attributes both his and Timothy's ability to endure suffering without denying the faith to the "power" of God. Who or what is this power, and how might we experience it?

Day 6

2 Timothy 1:9–12a

READ

... who saved us and called us to a holy calling, not because of our works but because of his own purpose and grace, which he gave us in Christ Jesus before the ages began, and which now has been manifested through the appearing of our Savior Christ Jesus, who abolished death and brought life and immortality to light through the gospel, for which I was appointed a preacher and apostle and teacher, which is why I suffer as I do.

MEDITATE

As we saw in the previous meditation, the power to overcome shame comes from knowing the truth of what the gospel alone can do: it saves otherwise hell-deserving sinners. This leads Paul, in verses 9–12a, to delineate the precise cause and nature of our salvation, which he does in four parts.

First, Paul refers to *what* God has done: "he saved us and called us to a holy calling" (v. 9a). Whatever the wide-ranging consequences of the gospel may be, its essence is delivering guilty sinners from eternal condemnation and reconciling them to God. The "call" by which we were brought into a saving relationship with God is the effectual drawing near that alone accounts for why we have come to believe (see John 6:37, 44; Rom 8:30). This is not the indiscriminate and universal invitation to believe in Christ but the work of the Spirit that actually secures a saving response on the part of God's elect. This call is holy because God, who is holy, is its author and because our holiness is its goal.

Second, Paul describes *why* God has done what he has done: it was "not because of our works but because of his own purpose and grace" (v. 9b). Clearly, "grace" and "works" stand in contrast. God's eternal purpose to save sinners is wholly of grace and not a response to the meritorious efforts, good intentions, or promises kept by men and women.

Third, Paul tells us *when* this gracious purpose occurred: it was "before the ages began" (v. 9c). This reinforces the fact that the cause of our salvation rests wholly in God (see Rom 9:10–11). What happens in time, when we are called to faith in Christ, is the outworking of a decision God graciously made before the foundation of the world (Eph 1:4). This eternal purpose is not arbitrary, as if God acted capriciously and without reason. His decision was according to, or based upon, his own purpose and grace. We are not informed as to what shapes God's purpose, other than that it is to magnify his grace and mercy. And with that we must remain satisfied.

Fourth, Paul explains *how* God did it: it was "through the appearing of our Savior Jesus Christ, who abolished death and brought life and immortality to light through the gospel" (v. 10). Here we see the execution in time of God's eternal purpose or decree. Christ's appearing had both a destructive and constructive effect. Destructively, Jesus abolished death. We who were spiritually dead were "made alive together with Christ"

(Eph 2:5). Constructively, the "life and immortality" brought by Christ assures us that one day our bodies will be raised and glorified to be like the glorious body of Jesus himself (Phil 3:20–21).

It was to proclaim this astounding truth that Paul was called as an apostle (Rom 1:1–2) and for the sake of this glorious gospel that he willingly endured shame and reproach and now calls on Timothy (and us all) to join him in suffering (2 Tim 1:12a).

REFLECT ON CHRIST

All through this opening paragraph in 2 Timothy we see the Christocentric focus of the gospel Paul preached. We have been included in God's eternal election unto life "in Christ Jesus" (v. 9b). Outside of Christ Jesus and his redemptive work on the cross, there is no hope for the forgiveness of sins. This marvelous salvation was manifested "through the appearing of our Savior Christ Jesus" (v. 10a). There is no other figure in human history who came to earth with the express purpose of securing eternal life for sinful men and women. It is only because the eternally preexistent Word of God (John 1:1) "became flesh and dwelt among us" (John 1:14) that we have any hope of life in the new heavens and new earth. It is Jesus and only Jesus who abolished death and provided the gift of immortality. No other religious figure, no other military commander, no other wise sage could ever accomplish what Christ alone has accomplished.

Neither the pressure of persecution nor the charge of arrogant elitism should deter us from the confession that eternal life is found only by grace alone, through faith alone, in Christ alone.

APPLY GOD'S WORD

The gospel of Jesus Christ is far more than merely good news. It is the very best news to be loudly proclaimed to a lost and dying world. What Paul describes in this paragraph is not intended to fuel wild speculation about why God chooses to do what he does. Its purpose is to awaken in us profoundly passionate gratitude for his grace and to energize us to make known to others the only path to forgiveness and eternal bliss.

Paul will soon remind us that "all who desire to live a godly life in Christ Jesus will be persecuted" (2 Tim 3:12). There is only one thing that will sustain otherwise weak and timid souls in the face of such suffering, and that is the gospel of what God has graciously done for us in and through the appearing of Jesus Christ. When faced with ridicule or exclusion or other forms of mistreatment, the power to remain steadfast will only come as we reflect on the eternal mercy shown to us in Christ Jesus. Willpower alone will never see us through hardship and trial. It is only the truth of the gospel that empowers the soul to rejoice in suffering.

PRAY

Eternally gracious God, awaken my heart to the marvelous grace you have showered upon me in Jesus. Open the eyes of my heart that I might see and savor the life that is mine forever because of what Jesus has done. And stir me to fervent praise as I reflect on the gift that I could never have earned on my own. Amen.

STUDY IT FURTHER

1. If the calling of God on our lives is described as "holy," what does this say about people who profess to believe in Christ but whose behavior is decidedly "unholy"? How would you respond to someone whose daily actions were in perpetual conflict with this verbal profession of faith?

2. Read Ephesians 2:8–10. What does it mean that we are not saved by works, but neither are we saved without them? What role do good works play in our relationship with God?

3. Read Ephesians 1:4–5. What does it tell you about the origin and cause of your salvation that it was decided in eternity past?

Day 7

2 Timothy 1:12b

READ

But I am not ashamed, for I know whom I have believed,
and I am convinced that he is able to guard until that day
what has been entrusted to me.

MEDITATE

Paul knew the pressure that comes with openly testifying to the gospel of Jesus. He undoubtedly felt the sting of ridicule, mockery, and rejection during the course of his ministry. The temptation to recoil in shame for being identified with Jesus was powerful. To remain silent was much safer, and the allure of being accepted and applauded, rather than humiliated, was intense. But the apostle refused to capitulate. Once again, echoing his appeal to Timothy in verse 8, Paul declares he is not ashamed (v. 12b). His suffering, noted again in verse 12a, exerted tremendous pressure on Paul to cower and keep his mouth shut, but he found the spiritual strength to remain faithful and resolved not to back down in bearing witness to "the testimony about our Lord" (v. 8). How did he do this? From where or from whom did this courage come?

Paul gives the answer in verse 12b: "I know whom I have believed, and I am convinced that he is able to guard until that day what has been entrusted to me." The strength to withstand the temptation to compromise or back off is found in a person: Jesus Christ. It was Paul's abiding and unshakable knowledge of Jesus that sustained him. He doesn't say it was "what" he knew that empowered his determination to preach but "whom" he knew: Jesus. And it isn't simply Jesus, but his power, his ability, the omnipotent commitment Jesus made to Paul (and to every believer) to "guard" what has been entrusted to us.

The latter half of verse 12 literally reads: "he is able to guard my deposit." There are two possible ways of understanding this statement: (1) The "deposit" may be what Paul has entrusted to God, be that his soul, his faith in Christ, his earthly ministry, his eternal reward, or something similar—his use of the possessive pronoun "my" supports this view. Or, (2) the "deposit" is what God has entrusted to Paul, probably a reference to the gospel. This second view is likely the correct one, given that the phrase "what has been entrusted" is the rendering of a single Greek word that appears only twice elsewhere in the New Testament. In both texts (1 Tim 6:20; 2 Tim 1:14), it clearly refers to a deposit or treasure that God has committed or entrusted to Timothy (1 Tim 6:20; 2 Tim 1:14). Timothy is the subject of the verb "to guard" in both of those verses: he is to guard what God has deposited with him, whereas in 2 Timothy 1:12 God (or Christ) is the one who guards the deposit.

Paul's point, then, is that when the day of Christ's return and the final judgment comes, he is assured that the gospel will be triumphant and vindicated in the sight of its enemies. It will have accomplished all that God designed for it, namely, the salvation of his elect people.

REFLECT ON CHRIST

Paul's confidence in the power of Christ must be noted. Often in Scripture the power or ability of the Lord is emphasized. Jesus asked the two blind men, "Do you believe that I am *able* to do this?" (Matt 9:28). The father of a demonized boy said to Jesus, "If you *can* do anything, have compassion on us and help us" (Mark 9:22). Jesus responded by saying, "'If you *can*'! All things are possible for one who believes" (Mark 9:23). Evidently, he means if you believe that he *can* do this, it will be done for you. Although well beyond child-bearing years, Abraham "grew strong in his faith as he gave glory to God, fully convinced that God was *able* to do what he had promised" (Rom 4:20–21). Abraham was willing to offer up Isaac as a sacrifice because "he considered that God was *able* even to raise him from the dead" (Heb 11:19). And in a famous doxology, Paul declares: "Now to him who is *able* to do far more abundantly than all that we ask or think, according to the power at work within us ..." (Eph 3:20; see also Rom 16:25; Jude 24).

Simply put, we can trust our Lord to do whatever he has promised to do. His ability is never in question.

APPLY GOD'S WORD

Consider what Paul's statement in verse 12 tells us about the person of Jesus Christ and our relationship to him. Paul focuses on three realities: his personal knowledge of Jesus ("I know" him and "have believed" him), the trustworthiness of the one whom he knows ("I am convinced"), and the ability of Jesus to do whatever is necessary to ensure that the gospel succeeds in the purpose God ordained for it ("he is able").

As noted earlier, Paul doesn't speak of knowing some abstract truth but of knowing Christ. His confidence is in the person of his Savior, his character, his reliability, his power, and not merely truths about him. Paul is altogether persuaded that Christ can be trusted to do what he has promised. Is your trust in him rooted in the ability or power of the Lord to guard, protect, and preserve the gospel as you, like Paul, make it known? Do you live in the grip of uncertainty and doubt, or do you know and have confidence in Christ that he will never fall short of fulfilling his word? Ponder the person of Jesus. Reflect on his commitment to uphold his people and make good on his promises.

PRAY

Lord, help me to overcome all hesitation and anxiety about your trustworthiness. Awaken my heart to your unlimited power and your unwavering commitment to the truth of the gospel. Banish from my mind all doubts and fill me with joyful confidence in your determination to be faithful to all you've promised. Amen.

STUDY IT FURTHER

1. When Paul says he *knows* the one he believes, what sort of knowledge does he have in mind: intellectual, confident trust, love, or some combination of these?

2. "Belief" is a word Christians often use but rarely define. What is the nature of our belief in Christ? What is the nature of saving faith?

3. Read 1 Peter 1:4–5. Compare what Peter says about our being "guarded through faith" with Paul's statement that God will "guard" what he has entrusted to us. Are these the same or different?

Day 8

2 Timothy 1:13–14

READ

Follow the pattern of the sound words that you have heard from me, in the faith and love that are in Christ Jesus. By the Holy Spirit who dwells within us, guard the good deposit entrusted to you.

MEDITATE

One of the more distressing trends in our day is the diminishing importance that pastors and average believers place on Christian doctrine. To say that this is a deviation from the priorities of Paul in particular and the New Testament in general is an understatement. Paul's exhortation to Timothy in verses 13–14 is unmistakable. A precious treasure, a deposit of immeasurable value has been entrusted to men like Timothy, and it must be guarded and protected from compromise or alteration at all costs.

The verb translated "follow" is the somewhat mundane Greek word "to have" or "to hold," but here the apostle has in mind a tenacious and rigorous holding to, embracing of, and active following after the truths revealed in Scripture, in particular the gospel itself. These truths constitute a distinctive body of beliefs that Paul

his letter to the Colossians. There he portrays his toiling for the gospel and the sake of the church as a "struggling with all his energy that he powerfully works within me" (Col 1:29). Paul knew that whatever degree of success he might attain in his apostolic ministry was not due to his education, native talents, or charismatic personality. He attributed everything to the powerful, energetic presence of the Spirit within. And he is determined to make certain that Timothy likewise draws upon the only source of strength that will enable him to faithfully fulfill the ministry to which he has been called. The same is true for you and me. May God grant us the power to walk in faithful, loving ministry to the glory of Jesus Christ.

PRAY

Father, I am weak, but you are strong. Impart to me and infuse my heart and mind with the powerful working of your Holy Spirit that I may faithfully guard and clearly make known the glory of the gracious gospel of what you have accomplished through your Son, and our Savior, Jesus Christ. Amen.

STUDY IT FURTHER

1. Paul speaks of a "pattern of the sound words" that we have received from God. In light of this, how would you respond to someone who downplays the importance of orthodoxy and sound doctrine? Just how important are these elements to our faith?

2. On the one hand, Paul says it is God who "guards" what he has entrusted to us. On the other, he exhorts Timothy to "guard" the good deposit. How do these two relate? Who is ultimately responsible for the safekeeping of our faith in Christ?

3. The fact that God has entrusted the glorious gospel to our care is sobering. What are you doing on a daily basis to guard it and promote it?

Day 9

2 Timothy 1:15–18

READ

You are aware that all who are in Asia turned away from me, among whom are Phygelus and Hermogenes. May the Lord grant mercy to the household of Onesiphorus, for he often refreshed me and was not ashamed of my chains, but when he arrived in Rome he searched for me earnestly and found me—may the Lord grant him to find mercy from the Lord on that day!—and you well know all the service he rendered at Ephesus.

MEDITATE

Paul knew from personal experience both the sting of betrayal and the healing balm of faithful, loyal service to his many needs. Both are described in this paragraph. Once again, the shame associated with Paul's imprisonment is seen in this text. This is why the apostle encouraged Timothy as he did earlier in verse 8. It would appear that the people in Asia who "turned away" from Paul, among whom were two men Paul chooses to identify (Phygelus and Hermogenes), did so because of their fear of being associated with someone in chains (v. 16). Onesiphorus, on the other hand, was not ashamed of Paul's arrest and incarceration or of the ignominy that such an experience undoubtedly brought upon the apostle.

Contrary to what some have suggested, verses 15–18 are not unrelated to what has preceded. In fact, it is here that Paul provides Timothy with personal examples of both cowardice and courage in gospel ministry. Paul tells him not to follow the example of Phygelus and Hermogenes; instead, he urges him to look to the bravery and self-sacrifice of Onesiphorus.

The leading Christians in Asia had decided to ignore Paul's appeal that they come to Rome and speak in his defense, or at a minimum, grant him the personal comfort of companionship and fellowship. Out of fear and shame, they all, save one, "turned away" (v. 15a). Did these people apostatize from the faith altogether (see 2 Tim 4:4; Titus 1:14), or did they abandon Paul personally but not their commitment to Christ? We can't be sure, but the latter is more likely.

We don't know why Paul singled out Phygelus and Hermogenes, but it seems reasonable to conclude that their defection was extraordinarily distressing to the apostle. Perhaps this is because they were leaders in the church or had been especially close to Paul. In either case, their turning away from him in his time of great need was shocking and undoubtedly quite painful.

Onesiphorus, on the other hand, proved remarkably loyal to Paul. Four things are said of him. We will note them in reverse order, which provides us with the order of events as they actually occurred. First, he served the church in Ephesus (v. 18). Second, he eagerly, and probably at great risk to his life, searched for Paul in Rome until finding him

(v. 17). Third, he refreshed Paul by his presence, perhaps bringing him much needed food, drink, and clothing (v. 16). Fourth, unlike the others from Asia, he was not ashamed of Paul's chains (v. 16).

This is why Paul prays that mercy be shown to Onesiphorus. The burden on his household or family must also have been extensive, and Paul prays that they too may be granted mercy from the Lord (v. 16). Contrary to what Roman Catholicism contends, there is no indication that Onesiphorus had passed away by the time of this writing, and thus no basis for thinking that Paul's request is an example of prayers for the dead. His prayer is for mercy to be shown on the day of judgment.

REFLECT ON CHRIST

What accounts for the selfless devotion of Onesiphorus and that of his extended family? We aren't told explicitly his motivation for the service he rendered to Paul, but it stands to reason that this man and his household were intensely committed to Christ Jesus and the spread of the gospel. Paul earlier referred to "the promise of the life that is in Christ Jesus" (v. 1), a blessing that constitutes the essence of the gospel or "good deposit" (v. 14) that Paul calls on Timothy to guard. Onesiphorus had himself tasted the sweetness of new life in Christ and was equally devoted to making whatever sacrifice was called for to spread this glorious good news.

This passage, then, is not primarily about Onesiphorus or his family. It is about the beauty and majesty of the Lord Jesus Christ who alone could awaken and sustain in the heart of this man and his household a commitment that would ignore danger, financial loss, and the very real possibility of imprisonment. Onesiphorus undertook this rigorous journey only secondarily for Paul. His primary aim was to contribute to the spread of the gospel of Christ Jesus and the glory of the one who had already shown him saving mercy.

APPLY GOD'S WORD

This is an opportune time for us to pause and probe deeply our own hearts to determine how serious we are about the person of Christ and the good deposit he has entrusted to us. Do we think primarily about what commitment to the Lord will cost us, what we might lose or forfeit or have confiscated should we remain faithful? Or is Christ Jesus of sufficient worth and value that not even life itself can compare with knowing him and making him known?

Paul made this calculation and drew only one conclusion. Notwithstanding the tremendous earthly accomplishments and accolades that came his way, he counted all such "gain" as loss "for the sake of Christ" (Phil 3:7). It was the "surpassing worth" or the supreme excellency or the unparalleled joy and satisfaction of "knowing Christ Jesus" as Lord that gave him the strength to suffer "the loss of all things" and to "count them as rubbish" (Phil 3:8).

Timothy also knew this to be true in his life, just as Onesiphorus did. Likewise, the family of Onesiphorus was prepared to forfeit everything for the sake of the gospel. Are you?

PRAY

Gracious God and heavenly Father, my prayer is that you would, by your Spirit, shine a light into my heart of the knowledge of the surpassing treasure that is Jesus himself. Guard me against cowering in shame and give me boldness to stand for the gospel, no matter the cost. Amen.

STUDY IT FURTHER

1. Paul was obviously abandoned by some who had pledged their loyalty to him. Have you experienced this in your relationships? If so, how did you respond? Did you become bitter and resentful, or did it thrust you even deeper into the arms of your heavenly Father?

2. Earlier in 2 Timothy 1 Paul repeatedly urged Timothy not to be ashamed of his imprisonment or suffering. Onesiphorus was clearly unashamed and was willing to suffer with Paul, if needed. Have you been faced with a similar challenge? How did you respond?

3. It would appear that Onesiphorus had the spiritual gift of serving, perhaps also mercy. Have you experienced this gifting in your own life? Even if you haven't, all Christians are responsible to serve others. Are there particular obstacles that hinder you from doing so?

Day 10

2 Timothy 2:1–2

READ

You then, my child, be strengthened by the grace that is in Christ Jesus, and what you have heard from me in the presence of many witnesses entrust to faithful men, who will be able to teach others also.

MEDITATE

The transitional conjunction "then" or "therefore" (*oun*) is important in verse 1. It may be that Paul is building his argument in chapter 2 based on what he said in 1:14, or perhaps he has in mind all of the first chapter, but his point would be: "Timothy, in light of all that I've just said about the importance of defending and suffering for the gospel, heed my counsel." Paul wanted to alert Timothy to the importance of what he says here as evidenced by the emphatic "you" with which verse 1 opens. It's as if he is saying, "You, Timothy, my spiritual child, as over against the defectors from Asia who turned away from me, pay heed to my words."

Paul does not tell Timothy to strengthen himself or to grow strong, as if the needed power is inherent within him, but to "be strengthened" (passive imperative) by the grace that is in Jesus ("by" reflects the instrumental use of the preposition "in" [*en*]). This is virtually identical to Paul's exhortation in Ephesians 6:10 that we "be strong in the Lord and in the strength of his might." It is also a reminder, once again, that grace is not only a principle but a power, the very energizing presence of Christ Jesus and the Spirit within us. In other words, we should actively feed on and draw from that reservoir of divine power that is made available by reason of our oneness with Christ.

The treasure and truth of the gospel is not something to be hidden away in Timothy's heart but must be transmitted to those who have already proven themselves faithful and committed. "What you have heard" has in view the whole counsel of God, including the many doctrinal truths and ethical principles that Paul himself faithfully communicated both in speech and writing. These were not private communications but were heard "in the presence of many witnesses."

Here we see the way in which the authoritative teaching of the apostles is transmitted to subsequent generations. It comes in four stages. First, it originated with Christ and was entrusted to Paul (2 Tim 1:12; see also Gal 1:11–12). Second, Paul in turn communicated the gospel to Timothy (2 Tim 1:13–14; 2:2). Third, Timothy is now called on to transmit these truths to faithful men (2 Tim 2:2, most likely qualified male elders; see Titus 1:5–9), who, fourth, are themselves "to teach others also" (2 Tim 2:2b). (Women, too, can receive the gift of teaching and are exhorted by Paul in Titus 2:3–5 to faithfully make use of this gift in teaching other women. [See also Acts 18:24–26].)

This is not a succession of persons or the passing down of spiritual authority attached to an office but transmission of the truth of the gospel that by God's providence is now given to us in the canonical Scriptures.

REFLECT ON CHRIST

We have seen repeatedly thus far in 2 Timothy how everything that we have in terms of both truth and salvation are found exclusively and sufficiently in Christ Jesus. Paul is an apostle "of Christ Jesus" (1:1). The promise of eternal life is found only "in Christ Jesus" (1:1). The grace, mercy, and peace we so desperately need come from the Father and "Christ Jesus our Lord" (1:2). God gave us saving grace in eternity past "in Christ Jesus" (1:9). It is through the appearing of "our Savior Christ Jesus" that salvation has broken into history (1:10), through whom also death has been abolished and life bestowed (1:10). It is in the faith and love "that are in Christ Jesus" (1:13) that we are to follow the pattern of sound words.

Now, Paul locates "in Christ Jesus" (2:1) the source of the spiritual strength that we all so desperately need to be empowered to resist the temptation to shrink back in shame. Suffering for the gospel is a high calling that can only be achieved by the energizing grace of Christ Jesus operating in us to sustain, encourage, and motivate us to remain faithful to the truth.

APPLY GOD'S WORD

We are, by nature, people who are inclined either to passivity or self-reliance. If we do overcome the former and engage in the spiritual battle that surrounds us, we often try to succeed in the power of our own will and ingenuity. Paul is making it clear in the opening verses of chapter 2 that the Christian life should never be distilled to a "let go and let God" mentality. Effortless Christianity is a contradiction. Holiness never just happens.

But when it does happen, it is always the fruit of the gracious empowering presence of Jesus and the work of the Holy Spirit. The life of a disciple of Jesus is a cross-bearing one, a race to be run, and a battle to be fought, all in the strength supplied by the risen Savior. If Paul had said to Timothy, "be strengthened," without directing him to the sole, sufficient, resourceful Savior in whom all empowering grace is found, his words would have fallen uselessly to the ground along with Timothy. We must never forget that everything we need to live a genuinely Christ-exalting life is found in Christ Jesus, and in Christ Jesus alone.

PRAY

Lord, forgive me for thinking that the Christian life to which you have called me lies in the power of my native talents. Grant me your sustaining mercy. Strengthen me by the energy that the grace of Christ Jesus alone can supply. Amen.

STUDY IT FURTHER

1. Read Romans 16:25–27 where Paul praises God who strengthens us according to the gospel. In 2 Timothy 2:1, he notes Timothy's weakness and his need for the empowering that only God's grace in the gospel can provide. In what ways does the grace of God empower us?

2. How does one judge whether a person is "faithful" in the sense that Paul has in mind? Does he mean faithful to God, to one another, to the church, or to something or someone else?

3. The faithful men mentioned must be able to teach others. The ability to teach is a requirement for someone to be an elder (1 Tim 3:2), but merely having a teaching gift does not

itself qualify one to be an elder. What constitutes this ability to teach? Must one be well-informed in the Scriptures? Must one be articulate in communicating biblical truths? What other factors are involved in this gifting?

Day 11

2 Timothy 2:3–6

READ

Share in suffering as a good soldier of Christ Jesus. No soldier gets entangled in civilian pursuits, since his aim is to please the one who enlisted him. An athlete is not crowned unless he competes according to the rules. It is the hard-working farmer who ought to have the first share of the crops.

MEDITATE

Paul's exhortation to Timothy to "share in suffering" has no explicit object or reference to the person(s) with whom he is to share this experience, but given what was said in 1:8 and 12, Paul would surely include himself and all other believers who contend for the gospel in this group.

Some may be surprised that Paul describes a follower of Jesus as a soldier (v. 3). The militaristic image this evokes seems to run counter to the rest of the New Testament, but there are all sorts of battles in which one may partake and thus a variety of roles for soldiers. Paul certainly does not intend for Timothy or any other believer to take up physical weaponry to advance the kingdom of God (see John 18:36). There is undoubtedly a war to wage, but as Paul elsewhere said, "The weapons of our warfare are not of the flesh but have divine power to destroy strongholds" (2 Cor 10:4). Likewise, in Ephesians 6:13–18 Paul encourages believers to adorn themselves with the armor of God, all of which is of a spiritual nature.

Paul proceeds to illustrate by means of three metaphors the nature of the demands and the rigors of the Christian life. The servant of Christ is to be as the soldier who is single-minded in his loyalty (v. 4), as the athlete whose success is entirely dependent on self-discipline (v. 5), and as the farmer whose hard work brings a fruitful harvest both for herself and others (v. 6).

Let's look more closely at each of these images. First, there is nothing intrinsically wrong about the daily, routine affairs of life until they entangle and distract us from our primary calling as soldiers of Christ. If mundane tasks absorb too much time and reshape our priorities so that we have no margin or energy left to "please" (v. 4) our commander in chief ("the one who enlisted" us), they must be set aside.

Second, Paul turns from the analogy of a Roman soldier to that of a Greek athlete. Single-minded devotion is essential but never enough. Just as in the Olympic games, so too in the Christian life there are God-given rules that must be followed if the gold medal is to be awarded.

Third, much like the first two images that Paul portrays, if the farmer is to reap a bountiful and fruitful harvest, she must expend all her energy in tilling the soil, planting her seed, and harvesting the crop. Of course, all this is to be understood in the light of the strength that only Christ's grace can provide (v. 1). Paul is not hesitant to call the people of God to fight, run, and labor for the sake of the gospel, but he is equally adamant that it must never be undertaken in the power of our own will and talents.

REFLECT ON CHRIST

Our Lord has called on us to engage in the battle with the world, the flesh, and the devil with single-minded commitment, law-abiding obedience, and strenuous effort. In doing so we must never lose sight of the one for whom we strive. It is as good soldiers of Christ Jesus that we fight and run and toil. His glory is the goal. His praise is the aim. Joyful satisfaction in him alone is our great reward.

If our motivation for heeding these exhortations is personal fame or monetary gain, it will all be for naught. We should at all times have it in our hearts to please the Lord, not ourselves or others whose approval we might be tempted to desire.

APPLY GOD'S WORD

The Christian life is not a casual stroll toward some heavenly realm. As J. C. Ryle once said, there are no "spiritual gains without pains." This is not to advocate for a works-oriented approach to Christian living, as if the cumulative effect of our good deeds could win the approval of God. At the same time, the Lord has called us to a focused, relentless, God-glorifying dedication to the revelation of his will as found in Scripture.

There is no place for quietism or pious passivity in our relationship with Jesus. Yes, we rest in his goodness and enjoy sweet fellowship as we meditate deeply on all that God is for us in Jesus. But this, too, calls for grace-empowered devotion and self-sacrificial commitment. We must never lose sight of the delicate balance established by God between a salvation that is by grace alone, through faith alone, and not of works and the fact that "we are his workmanship, created in Christ Jesus for good works, which God prepared beforehand, that we should walk in them" (Eph 2:10).

PRAY

God, I confess that I am weak and that you are strong. I know all too well that I am often cowardly and desperately in need of the courage that only you can provide. Equip and empower me so that I may overcome my lazy and misguided approach to Christian living, and help me focus instead on doing all that is pleasing to you. Amen.

STUDY IT FURTHER

1. In light of Paul's repeated emphasis on suffering for the sake of the gospel, is this something that only apostles will experience or is it an inevitable reality that all Christians in every age should embrace? Are there exceptions?

2. It is easy for us to get entangled in earthly matters. How could one avoid the trap of being so wrapped up in the mundane affairs of life that one's commitment to Christ is undermined?

3. How do we avoid concluding from this text that good works are the basis for our salvation? How can we strive to compete to win without cheapening the grace of God?

Day 12

2 Timothy 2:7

READ

Think over what I say, for the Lord will give you understanding in everything.

MEDITATE

In 2 Timothy 2:7, Paul provides his spiritual son with a crucial word of counsel. His reference to "what I say" most likely encompasses the entirety of what is found in this epistle, as well as what Paul wrote elsewhere and spoke to Timothy in face-to-face conversations, and not just what has preceded in this one epistle. Paul has already referred to "the pattern of the sound words" that he has communicated to Timothy (2 Tim 1:13), and in 2:1–2 he exhorts his protégé to transmit to faithful men "what you have heard from me."

There are three things to be noted in this one verse. First is the *command* to "think over what I say" (v. 7a). Second, there is a *promise* that "the Lord will give you understanding in everything." And third, we must not overlook the *relationship* between the command and the promise as indicated by the word "for" (*gar*).

Some may feel a tension between the command to "think" and the promise that God will provide insight into the meaning of Paul's words. Sadly, many use the promise as an excuse to ignore the command: "If God is going to give me understanding in everything, I don't need to think. I only need to wait passively until the Spirit illumines my heart." This way of responding to Paul's command breeds anti-intellectualism and a neglect of the importance of propositional revelation in Scripture.

More important still, this approach fails to note the significant causal relationship ("for") between the two elements in Paul's statement. Paul's point is that we are to think, study, and dig deeply into the word because God will give us understanding. In other words, illumination is the fruit of investigation. The former doesn't preclude need of the latter. The latter is the pathway to the former. Should we pray for divine illumination? Of course! Should we expect God to give us understanding? Absolutely. But only as and after we have thought about what the text says.

The Spirit's ministry of illumination does not replace the human work of meditation on God's word. We can't afford to presume that the promise of divine light and understanding is given to everyone. It is promised to those who commit to thinking. Praying and thinking are not mutually exclusive options. The person who only thinks and does not pray is as dangerous and unbalanced as the person who only prays and never thinks. Yes, God has promised to illumine our minds and spirits, to disclose and reveal the secrets of his heart and ways, but he promises to do this through and in response to our diligent devotion to studying and understanding the biblical text.

We should also take note of the delicate balance here between the sovereignty of God and human responsibility. Clearly Paul expected Timothy to exercise his cognitive powers, to apply himself to the things that Paul had spoken about by inspiration of the Spirit, with complete confidence that in and through his obedience to that task God through the Holy Spirit would speak and enlighten and convict and reveal his heart to him.

REFLECT ON CHRIST

The promise in 2 Timothy 2:7 most likely speaks to the work of the Holy Spirit in disclosing to us the person of Christ as well as the significance of his words. Jesus promised that "when the Spirit of truth comes, he will guide you into all the truth, for he will not speak on his own authority, but whatever he hears he will speak, and he will declare to you the things that are to come. He will glorify me, for he will take what is mine and declare it to you. All that the Father has is mine; therefore I said that he will take what is mine and declare it to you" (John 16:13–15).

Timothy was not present in the upper room when Jesus gave this promise, but it would apply to him just as it did to the Twelve. Paul spoke elsewhere of this work of spiritual enlightenment in his prayer on behalf of the Ephesians (and not just the apostolic company). He prays "that the God of our Lord Jesus Christ, the Father of glory, may give you the Spirit of wisdom and of revelation in the knowledge of him, having the eyes of your hearts enlightened" (Eph 1:17–18a). Let us embrace the certainty of the promise, but only as we obey the command on which its fulfillment is based.

APPLY GOD'S WORD

As noted briefly above, there are many in the body of Christ who recoil at the thought of devoting themselves to the careful and meticulous study of God's written word. They have been led to believe that such an intellectual exercise will breed either arrogance or some form of religious legalism. After all, didn't

Paul say that "'knowledge' puffs up" (1 Cor 8:1)? No one wants to be accused of being a Pharisee.

Others, at the far end of the spectrum, take pride in their cognitive grasp of biblical truth and fail to rely on the illumination and quickening work of the Spirit by which he enables us to understand, love, and respond to the written truth of Scripture. Paul's exhortation and promise in 2 Timothy 2:7 is a much needed reminder to us to embrace both the authority of the written word and the enlightening work of the Holy Spirit, both truth and power.

PRAY

Father, I am so desperately needy for the insight and understanding that you alone can provide. I pray that as I immerse myself in your word and all that you have revealed of yourself and your purpose in Christ Jesus that you would, by the Holy Spirit, quicken my mind, bring conviction to my heart, stir my spirit, and grant me to see and understand your glorious truth. I confess that I am by nature dull and selfish and stand in great need of the enlightening work that only you can accomplish. Amen.

STUDY IT FURTHER

1. Why do some Christians suppose that thinking is detrimental to their personal relationship with Christ? What is the cause of anti-intellectualism in the church today?

2. This is a call to serious reflection and meditation on what is revealed to us in Scripture. How does this sort of thinking avoid the pitfalls of Eastern meditation? On what should our thinking and reflecting be focused?

3. What advice would you give to a believer who chooses only to think and to rely entirely on their intellectual prowess? What are the dangers of an overly intellectual approach to Christianity?

Day 13

2 Timothy 2:8

READ

Remember Jesus Christ, risen from the dead, the offspring of David, as preached in my gospel …

MEDITATE

Observe both what Paul says and doesn't say. He doesn't say "remember Jesus Christ," or even "remember Jesus who rose from the dead." Neither does he say "remember the resurrection of which Jesus is the first to experience." He doesn't draw attention to our Lord's earthly life, his substitutionary death, or to any other event that in any other context would be perfectly permissible and helpful to mention.

Rather, he says: Remember Jesus *as the living Lord.* Remember him precisely in his identity as the one whom God raised from the dead and seated at his right hand in power and authority over all of creation. Keep in the forefront of your thinking and vividly present in your heart Jesus as the living Lord. He was raised and is even now still raised and will be forevermore (this brings out the full force of the perfect passive participle, literally translated, "having been raised," with the focus on an event in the past that has implications in the present and into the future). Paul's emphasis is on the resurrection as an ongoing, irreversible reality—a perpetual fact of space-time history.

This Jesus is "the offspring of David" (v. 8b). This is Paul's way of pointing to the incarnation and humanity of Jesus. This one who himself walked the earth and suffered abuse and slander and death on a cross is the one you must consistently remember and call to mind as risen from the dead. Paul wants to make sure Timothy knows that Jesus was human as well as divine. It was the Word, God the Son, not an angel, who was born of the seed of David and is now the living, reigning Lord over all. Of course, this reference to Jesus as the "offspring of David" is Paul's way of alerting his Jewish readers that this Jesus whom God raised from the dead is in fact the Messiah (Luke 1:31–33; Gal 4:4).

The bodily resurrection of Jesus is "as preached in my gospel" (v. 8b). The resurrection of Jesus is not tangential to the gospel but absolutely central to it. Without the reality of a risen Savior there is nothing good in the news that Paul preached. The good news of the gospel is that God, in raising Jesus from the dead, has overcome and triumphed over that relentless predator: death. The resurrection is the reason we can have confidence that what Jesus achieved in his life, ministry, and sacrificial death is true and lasting. In other words, of what possible good was Jesus's sinless life if he's dead and decaying? What authority could we possibly give to his teaching if he's ultimately no different from any other religious leader who died? And why would we ever believe that his death was atoning and has fully paid the penalty for our sin if he could not conquer the grave?

REFLECT ON CHRIST

Some would contend, incorrectly, that because Jesus was raised from the dead faithful servants such as Paul should not be in prison. How can we say that Jesus is the risen, living king over all things while his most preeminent apostle is languishing in chains in a filthy Roman dungeon on the verge of brutal execution?

This doesn't sound like good news if it is on account of that very news that Paul is "bound with chains as a criminal" (v. 9a). Should not the "good news" entail the assurance of freedom, prosperity, robust health, and physical comfort? Paul will answer this question in verse 10. There may well be suffering in this life for those who embrace and rely upon the gospel of Christ's resurrection, but it secures for them salvation with eternal glory in the ages to come.

Precisely because Paul was in prison and knew that he would never be released he directed Timothy's attention and ours as well to Christ as risen. He wanted Timothy to understand that no human demise, no earthly setback, no so-called crushing defeat at the hands of unbelievers could ever reverse God's purposes or undo the accomplishment of the cross. The reason why the word of God or the gospel is "not bound" (v. 9) but instead is flourishing is because the Christ, the Savior, of whom it speaks is very much alive.

APPLY GOD'S WORD

Paul wants Timothy to be strengthened to endure whatever hardships come his way by remembering that Christ has conquered every enemy, even death itself, and reigns as the living Lord over his life and all the adversity and painful circumstances he encounters. No matter how hard life may be or how serious your suffering may become, no matter how powerful the temptation to shrink back in shame, the most that anyone on this earth can do is kill you. So, remember Jesus as the risen and ruling Lord who has overcome death and has removed its sting. Remember what Jesus said: "Do not fear those who kill the body but cannot kill the soul" (Matt 10:28).

We must remember Jesus and think of him as the risen, reigning, almighty Savior and sovereign Lord over all mankind, even over those men and women who greatly ridicule us and reject us and seek to destroy us. Paul will later remind Timothy that if we hope to "reign with him" (2 Tim 2:12b) we must "endure" (2:12a) the mistreatment and misunderstanding that following Christ inevitably entails.

PRAY

Great God and sovereign Lord, impress on my heart that no amount of adversity, no imprisonment or execution at the hands of an unbelieving world, can separate me from the love you have for me in the risen, reigning Christ (Rom 8:38–39). Amen.

STUDY IT FURTHER

1. Jesus tells us to remember him whenever we partake of the elements of the Lord's Supper (1 Cor 11:25–26). Here Paul encourages us to remember Jesus as risen from the dead. How do we obey these commands? Is it merely a matter of thinking deeply, or is there more?

2. Why is preaching central to the gospel? Have we been faithful to the call of God if we refuse to verbally proclaim the gospel? What obstacles are there in your heart to boldly making known the saving grace of God in Christ?

3. Paul refers to the gospel as his ("my gospel"). Do you think of the gospel also as yours? In what sense has it been entrusted to you as it was entrusted to Paul?

Day 14

2 Timothy 2:9

READ

... for which I am suffering, bound with chains as a criminal. But the word of God is not bound!

MEDITATE

Paul's reference to being "bound with chains" calls for some comment. We need to understand the circumstances under which he found himself imprisoned in Rome.

Luke tells us of Paul's first Roman imprisonment in Acts 28. It was during that time that Paul wrote what we now call, somewhat mistakenly, the Prison Epistles (Ephesians, Philippians, Colossians, and Philemon). I say "mistakenly" because Paul's accommodations were not that oppressive. In Acts 28, Paul stayed in his own rented house (Acts 28:30), whereas in 2 Timothy he is in chains (2:9). During his first Roman imprisonment, he was surrounded by friends (Acts 28:17–31), whereas during the second he was virtually alone (only Luke was with him; 2 Tim 4:11). During the first imprisonment he was freely accessible to his friends (Acts 28:30) and anticipated his soon release (Phil 1:25–26; 2:24; Phlm 22), but during the second he was hard to locate (Onesiphorus finally succeeded), and he looked forward to almost certain execution (2 Tim 4:6–8).

So, how did Paul get from the relatively comfortable detainment described in Acts 28 to the more demanding imprisonment we read about in 2 Timothy? After Paul was released from his first Roman imprisonment, he went to Crete where he left behind Titus to appoint elders and set things in order (Titus 1:5). From there he traveled to Ephesus where he left Timothy for much the same reason (1 Tim 1:3–4). He proceeded to visit both Colossae and Philippi, and somewhere along the way, probably while in Macedonia, he wrote his first epistle to Timothy and the letter to Titus. When Paul finally made it to Rome, it would have been in the following spring.

It was about this time, in AD 64, that the fire of Rome broke out. The Roman emperor Nero needed a scapegoat on which to blame the debacle. He found it in the Christian community, as a result of which Paul was arrested (elsewhere, the word "criminal" is only used in Luke 23:32, 33, 39 to describe the thieves crucified with Jesus). Paul may have been in Troas when this occurred (see 2 Tim 4:13). He was likely beheaded on the Ostian Way, about three miles outside the city of Rome. It was perhaps only days, weeks at most, before his execution that Paul wrote his second letter to Timothy.

Knowing that he was about to die for his faith in Christ, Paul's final words to Timothy (and to us) are to be given serious consideration. There is no room or time left for frivolous arguments or what Paul refers to as "foolish, ignorant controversies" that breed only "quarrels" (2 Tim 2:23). This historical context should alert us to the urgency and importance of everything Paul says in this short epistle. It is with his final breath that the apostle issues these instructions, warnings, and assurances. May God alert us to the urgency of paying close attention.

Chains may bind the human body, but they have no effect on the divine message of God's saving power in the gospel. While Paul may languish in a dungeon, the truth of God's purpose in Christ Jesus will continue to spread and accomplish the goal for which it has been ordained.

REFLECT ON CHRIST

Paul's command at the beginning of 2 Timothy 2:8 should be read with the sense of vital importance that the apostle no doubt intended: "Remember Jesus Christ!" Imprisoned in a Roman dungeon, knowing full well that his earthly sojourn was nearing its end, the one enduring truth that sustained him, or perhaps we should say the one eternal person who stood by Paul and whom Paul wants Timothy to keep ever present in the forefront of his mind, is Jesus Christ.

As the chains chafed against his skin, as he reflected back on some thirty years of evangelistic outreach, church planting, and teaching, the one thing that made it all worthwhile was the glory, beauty, and majesty of the Lord Jesus Christ. Paul was decidedly Christocentric in his thinking, in his preaching, and in his perseverance in the midst of suffering. He could likely have secured his release and lived a long and fruitful life had he been willing to renounce Jesus. But he chose instead to remember him! And he urges Timothy and all believers to do the same. Were you or I ever to find ourselves in similar circumstances, I pray we would fix in the forefront of our souls the person of Jesus, risen from the dead.

APPLY GOD'S WORD

For most of us reading this devotional, our suffering is not akin to what Paul suffered in Rome. You may well be

Day 15

2 Timothy 2:10

READ

Therefore I endure everything for the sake of the elect, that they also may obtain the salvation that is in Christ Jesus, with eternal glory.

MEDITATE

Paul never viewed suffering as an end in itself, as if there were some special virtue in it. There was always a higher spiritual purpose in his willingness to undertake the sort of gospel ministry that invariably provoked his enemies and led to his imprisonment. If he suffered, he did so in order that those chosen by God ("the elect") might obtain that salvation to which they have been predestined (see Rom 8:29–30).

To believe in the Bible is to believe in election. It is a topic referred to numerous times in the New Testament. The verb "to choose" or "to elect" (*eklegomai*) is found twenty-two times in the New Testament, many of which refer to those elected to inherit eternal life (e.g., Mark 13:20; Acts 13:17; 1 Cor 1:27 [2x], 28; Eph 1:4; Jas 2:5). The noun "elect" (*eklektos*), found here in 2 Timothy 2:10, is also used twenty-two times in the

New Testament (see, e.g., Matt 22:14; 24:22, 24, 31; Mark 13:20, 22, 27; Luke 18:7; Rom 8:33; Col 3:12; Titus 1:1; 1 Pet 1:1; 2:9; 2 John 1, 13; Rev 17:14). The noun most often translated "election" (*eklogē*) is used seven times, all of which refer to salvation (Acts 9:15; Rom 9:11; 11:5, 7, 28; 1 Thess 1:4; 2 Pet 1:10). In addition, we could cite the variety of terms that mean "to predestine" (*proorizō*) or "to choose" (*haireō*) or "to appoint" (*tassō*). Clearly, though, the terms used in the New Testament do not of themselves tell us anything definitive about the basis of divine election. That issue must be determined by the way in which each term is used, as well as other relevant statements in each context.

The basis or grounds for God's election of individuals is unavoidably controversial. Some contend that God's pretemporal choice of some to be saved was conditional, being suspended upon his foreknowledge of their freewill response to the gospel. Others believe that had God made his decision based on how people would respond to the gospel, no one would be saved because no one would be either able or willing to embrace Christ in faith (see Rom 3:10–18). Thus, election was unconditional, its only basis being God's sovereign good pleasure (Rom 9:10–23). As Paul wrote to the Romans, election to eternal life "depends not on human will or exertion, but on God, who has mercy" (Rom 9:16).

Whereas some may argue that unconditional election undermines or renders superfluous human response, we see here in Paul's language a beautiful portrayal of the harmony between the sovereignty of God and human responsibility. Paul never concluded from the truth of unconditional election that nothing else was needed for those chosen to enter into life. His proclamation of the gospel to them that provoked his enemies to persecute and imprison him was the means by which, in accordance with God's plan, the elect were to experience the "eternal glory" (v. 10) that comes with the salvation that Christ Jesus has died to obtain. Had Paul not been willing to suffer, he wouldn't have preached the gospel. And if he hadn't preached the gospel, the elect would not have been saved. This mystery may not be fully understood, but it can never be denied.

REFLECT ON CHRIST

As we have seen over and again in 2 Timothy, Paul connects the salvation of individuals to Christ Jesus. This is an echo of Paul's comments in Ephesians 1:3–14 where he declares that every spiritual blessing we experience is "in Christ" (Eph 1:3) and that God chose us "in him" before the foundation of the world (Eph 1:4). We were predestined for adoption "through Jesus Christ" (Eph 1:5), in whom "we have redemption through his blood" (Eph 1:7). This altogether Christ-centered focus on the source and means of our salvation is found repeatedly in the New Testament.

Paul's declaration in 2 Timothy 2:10, that the salvation we obtain is "in Christ Jesus," is a summary of his thoughts in Ephesians. There is nothing of any benefit, spiritually or otherwise, that comes our way apart from who Christ is and all that he has so graciously accomplished for us in his life, death, and resurrection. The eternal glory that accompanies our salvation is itself the experience and enjoyment of the radiant beauty and majestic splendor of Christ. Paul elsewhere assures us that "when Christ who is your life appears, then you also will appear with him in glory" (Col 3:4).

APPLY GOD'S WORD

Knowing that by God's sovereign and gracious choice we are elected to eternal life should stir up at least four responses in us. First, we should react with awe and amazement at the unmerited and altogether undeserved blessing that God has bestowed on us. Simply put, election should lead us to worship him. Second, we should rejoice that we are among God's chosen. Jesus said to his disciples: "Nevertheless, do not rejoice in this, that the spirits are subject to you, but rejoice that your names are written in heaven" (Luke 10:20).

Third, gratitude should flood our hearts as we give thanks to God for this precious gift of eternal life. We must never be presumptuous or think that we were chosen because of something in us, produced by our own effort, that God could not find in others. Fourth, knowing that we are chosen, redeemed, and forgiven solely on the grounds of God's mercy should motivate us to service and obedience, all to the glory of the one who made us the objects of his eternal love.

PRAY

Righteous Father, I stand in awe of your amazing grace, that you would get the consent of your holy will to set your saving love on hell-deserving sinners like me. Awaken in my heart a commensurate sense of gratitude and joy for all that you have done to deliver me from a well-earned damnation. All praise be to your name! Amen.

STUDY IT FURTHER

1. Why is the doctrine of election so controversial? Where do you stand on this issue? Is God's saving choice of you based on his foreknowledge of your act of free will, or is it based solely on his sovereign good pleasure?

2. Does Paul's statement in this verse suggest that some of the elect may ultimately fail to obtain final salvation? If yes, why? If not, why not?

3. Read 2 Corinthians 4:16–18. Consider the contrast between Paul's current painful and distressing circumstances, on the one hand, and his hope of entering into eternal glory, on the other. How does reflecting on and hoping in the latter enable us to endure the former?

Day 16

2 Timothy 2:11–13

READ

The saying is trustworthy, for: "If we have died with him, we will also live with him; if we endure, we will also reign with him; if we deny him, he also will deny us; if we are faithless, he remains faithful"—for he cannot deny himself.

MEDITATE

The opening phrase in verse 11 literally reads, "Faithful is the saying ..." This phrase occurs five times in the New Testament, all in the Pastoral Epistles (see 1 Tim 1:15; 3:1; 4:9; 2 Tim 2:11; Titus 3:8). Twice it is expanded with the words "and deserving of full acceptance" (1 Tim 1:15; 4:9). This phrase introduces a theological slogan that had evidently gained currency in the early church and may well have been a portion of an evangelical hymn or confession of faith. In saying that such slogans are "trustworthy," Paul means they are unassailable and undeniable.

The force of the connecting term "for" in verse 11a is uncertain. Some believe that Paul now draws conclusions in light of what he just said in verse 10. But insofar as these statements in verses 11–13 are likely only a portion of a hymn or confession of faith circulating in the early church, "for" probably refers to something that preceded in the original writing. Still, though, we cannot overlook the connection of verses 11–13 with the preceding paragraph. In verses 4–7 we hear Paul's appeal for faithful endurance in Christian living. In verses 8–10 we read of election unto salvation and glory and the inevitable suffering that comes on those who proclaim the gospel. It would seem, then, that Paul's design for incorporating these well-known Christian sayings is to bolster his earlier call for faithful endurance and to provide Timothy with a motivation to stand fast along with a warning lest he be tempted to waver.

The saying has four lines: the first two speak positively with words of confidence; the third line speaks negatively, containing words of admonition and warning; and the fourth line is a combination—the first half speaks of disloyalty, the second of God's faithfulness in spite of it.

In the first line (v. 11b), the death envisioned is likely the spiritual death we are reckoned to have experienced in Christ when we came to saving faith (see Rom 6:1–5; Gal 2:20). The life that follows this death is both a present reality in that we are "alive to God in Christ Jesus" (Rom 6:11, 8) and have a future hope of bodily resurrection (Rom 6:5).

The second line (v. 12a) alludes to the endurance in suffering noted in verse 10, and the promise of reigning with Christ likely points to co-regency with him in the eternal state (see Rev 3:21).

To "deny" Christ is to repudiate his identity and our association with him, from which one may repent, as Peter did. Unlike Peter's response, in verse 12, this denial is a final, persistent, unrepentant rejection of Jesus that results in his denial of us (see Matt 10:32–33). The warning, therefore, is not addressed to a believer who might deny Christ and forfeit his salvation but envisions those whose professed faith is spurious (John 8:31–42; see also Heb 3:6, 14).

Finally, does being "faithless" refer to periodic failure to trust on our part (something we all experience), or to the sort of unrepentant repudiation of Christ as found in the third saying? Paul is most likely not asserting the possibility of apostasy but giving us a promise: even if we falter in our faith, God remains true to his character and his promises to the elect and will forgive us and keep us secure (Phil 1:6; 1 Pet 1:5).

It's important to remember that in verses 11–13 Paul employs the "preacher's 'we.' " He encompasses everyone in his promises and warnings, both elect and non-elect, and assures us that if *we* do this in relation to Christ, *we* will enjoy certain blessings, while if *we* do not, *we* will suffer the judicial consequences.

REFLECT ON CHRIST

Once again Paul grounds everything pertaining to our salvation in the person of Christ. To "die" with Christ points to our identification with him in his crucifixion. When he died, we are reckoned to have died. When he rose from the dead, we are so reckoned, all of which is expressed in the waters of baptism. This is Paul's point in Romans 6, where he asks the rhetorical question: "Do you not know that all of us who have been baptized into Christ Jesus were baptized into his death? We were buried with him by baptism into death, in order that, just as Christ was raised from the dead by the glory of the Father, we too might walk in newness of life" (Rom 6:3–4; see also Gal 3:27).

Peter's threefold denial of Jesus was grievous and cowardly, but he repented. And he did so because God had faithfully committed himself to uphold his elect child and restore Peter to repentance. Indeed, Jesus prayed for Peter's restoration: "But

I have prayed for you that your faith may not fail. And when you have turned again, strengthen your brothers" (Luke 22:32). Here we see both Peter's lack of faith and the unwavering faithfulness of Christ to uphold him.

APPLY GOD'S WORD

There is a delicate tension between the necessity of enduring, saving faith on the part of the elect, on the one hand, and the commitment of God to preserve them through faith, on the other. The latter does not undermine the former but guarantees it. It is only by virtue of God's commitment to bring to final fruition the saving work he initially began in us (Phil 1:6) that we are capable of continuing to trust Christ and not deny him.

The sort of warning that we see in 2 Timothy 2:11–13 may well be the very means by which God preserves us in faith. Hearing and heeding, by the power of the Spirit, the dire warning of what would happen should we deny Jesus as Lord, we are kept secure in our salvation. The threat is real, but the promise of God is that he will enable us to persevere until the final day. Hence Jude's praise of him "who is able to keep you from stumbling and to present you blameless before the presence of his glory with great joy" (Jude 24).

PRAY

O great Triune God, may I never presume upon my salvation or attribute my election and perseverance to anything other than your amazing mercy and grace. To you be all the glory and honor for eternal life! Amen.

STUDY IT FURTHER

1. This passage puts before us two truths: God's sovereignty and our responsibility. How do you reconcile what appears to be a contradiction between the two? How are they harmonious?

2. Read Revelation 2:26–27; 3:21. How do these texts help us understand what it means to "reign" with Christ? When, and in what way, will this "reign" occur?

3. Have there been occasions when you sensed that your silence was, in effect, a denial of Jesus? How did you respond? In what way does God's faithfulness and his commitment to himself sustain you through trials like this?

Day 17

2 Timothy 2:14–19

READ

Remind them of these things, and charge them before God not to quarrel about words, which does no good, but only ruins the hearers. Do your best to present yourself to God as one approved, a worker who has no need to be ashamed, rightly handling the word of truth. But avoid irreverent babble, for it will lead people into more and more ungodliness, and their talk will spread like gangrene. Among them are Hymenaeus and Philetus, who have swerved from the truth, saying that the resurrection has already happened. They are upsetting the faith of some. But God's firm foundation stands, bearing this seal: "The Lord knows those who are his," and, "Let everyone who names the name of the Lord depart from iniquity."

MEDITATE

Words are the building blocks on which the fundamental truths of Christianity are built. We must strive to be accurate in their use, but there is no excuse for arguing and dividing over trivial and ultimately destructive words. This serves no good purpose (cf. Eph 4:29), "but only ruins the hearers" (v. 14). "These things" (v. 14) about which Timothy is to remind his people are the collective truths already explained up to this point in the epistle, together with everything to follow. In doing so, Timothy must be careful to shun destructive word wars and wrangling over matters that are irrelevant to godly living. Such "irreverent babble" (v. 16) may give the appearance of high-minded concern for the truth, but it will only serve to lead people into ungodliness.

Paul wants Timothy to strive or hasten (*spoudazō*; lit., be zealous or eager) to show himself "approved" to God by "rightly handling the word of truth" (v. 15b). The verb *orthotomeō,* translated "rightly handling," has the sense of guiding along a straight path or to cut straight. In other words, he should be careful, accurate, clear, and forthright in the presentation of revealed truth. This demonstrates that in denouncing vain word games Paul is not minimizing the critical importance of properly interpreting and applying God's word.

Timothy is contrasted with two men, Hymenaeus and Philetus, whose heretical deviation from the truth entailed a denial of the future, physical, bodily resurrection of believers. Such an error had already undermined the faith of some in Ephesus. These two men probably argued that the only resurrection for believers was entirely spiritual in nature, having already taken place in the moment of regeneration by the Spirit. This may be an indication of an early, incipient form of gnosticism present in the church, according to which physical reality, especially the body, was viewed as evil.

But Timothy should not be shaken by the departure of such men, for the "elect" (v. 10) are known by the Lord as his precious possession. This is God's "seal" or guarantee that his chosen ones are known and secure. It's uncertain whether the "firm foundation" refers to God's act of electing his people to eternal life or to "the apostles and prophets" (Eph 2:20) on whose revelatory ministry the church is built. It may even be a reference to Christ Jesus, "the cornerstone" (Eph 2:20b), or perhaps to the elect themselves.

In any case, Paul wants to encourage Timothy not to be shaken by apostasy in the professing community. Even if we cannot always know who is truly saved, God can be trusted to discern those who are genuinely his, having predestined them to inherit life through the Son. If those who name "the name of the Lord" (v. 19) truly belong to God, they will refrain from iniquity. Such is both the outcome of belonging to God and the evidence that one is truly saved.

REFLECT ON CHRIST

The "Lord" mentioned twice in verse 19 is likely a reference to Jesus, although what he knows the Father and Spirit also know. This passage is an echo of several statements in the Gospel of John. There, Jesus is portrayed as "the shepherd of the sheep" who "calls his own sheep by name and leads them out" (John 10:2, 3). The good shepherd not only knows his sheep but "lays down his life" for them (John 10:11). Again, Jesus claims that as the good shepherd, "I know my own and my own know me" (John 10:14). This knowledge is an expression of intimacy and ownership. The elect of God, or the sheep of the good shepherd, are not an undifferentiated herd. Each individual is known and loved and cared for by the Lord Jesus.

This salvific knowledge or spiritual intimacy is mutual. Jesus will later in John's Gospel describe eternal life in these terms: "They know you, the only true God, and Jesus Christ whom you have sent" (John 17:3). Those who know God and have eternal life are the ones whom the Father gave to the Son "out of the world" (John 17:6). Clearly, then, these whom the

Father gave the Son, for whom the Son died, are intimately known by the Lord.

APPLY GOD'S WORD

All of us, at one time or another, experience the fear of being alone and anonymous. It is terrifying and depressing. But this is directly contrary to the purpose for which we were created. God's saving work in Jesus is designed to call out of darkness and into the light of intimacy and fellowship a people whom God knows personally. These are the elect—those fallen sinners who are sealed by the Spirit and secure in their relationship with God.

It is heartbreaking today, as it must undoubtedly have been for Timothy in the first century, to watch as men and women we believed had been born again apostatize. They may not deny the future bodily resurrection in the same way that Hymenaeus and Philetus did, but their defection from the faith and departure from the community of the church is their unmasking (see 1 John 2:19). But we may rest assured that God will never abandon his own. He knows us by name. Such is the firm foundation on which our salvation is built. Such is the seal of God on our lives.

PRAY

Lord, I confess that I am often deceived as to who truly knows you in a saving way. Grant me discernment. Grant me patience. But above all else, grant me joy and comfort in knowing that I am known as yours. Amen.

STUDY IT FURTHER

1. What are some of the useless arguments and "irreverent babble" that you have witnessed in the church? Was

there any spiritual benefit? How should you respond to others when they allow themselves to be caught up in such disputes?

2. Do you know how to rightly handle the word of truth? What are you doing to improve your skill in reading and interpreting the Scriptures? Why is our growth in the Christian life largely dependent on our facility with the written word of God?

3. Can you cite examples in your experience or in the life of your church where people have "swerved from the truth"? What were the results? What was done to help them return to the stability of the truth of God's word?

Day 18

2 Timothy 2:20–21

READ

Now in a great house there are not only vessels of gold and silver but also of wood and clay, some for honorable use, some for dishonorable. Therefore, if anyone cleanses himself from what is dishonorable, he will be a vessel for honorable use, set apart as holy, useful to the master of the house, ready for every good work.

MEDITATE

Let's examine the connection between these verses and the ones before. Paul has just spoken of the very real possibility of professing Christians swerving from the truth (v. 18). One can reasonably assume that he was describing apostasy, a wholesale abandonment of the faith. This is a serious matter, so he illustrates the point with an analogy.

The "great house" (v. 20a) is a reference to the visible, or professing, local church in which are both genuine believers and those whose alleged faith is spurious. The many vessels mentioned by Paul are the members of any particular church. These vessels (individual persons) differ as to value. Some are made of gold and silver while others are made of wood and clay. We must not press the analogy, as if Paul were saying that some people are of greater moral worth than others, as all are created in God's image. He is simply drawing on a distinction in the realm of physical matter to make the point that not everyone who professes faith in Christ truly knows the Lord. Not every professing believer in a local church is devoted to "honorable use."

Before proceeding, a parallel text may help elucidate what Paul is saying here. Most scholars believe that 2 Timothy and the shorter Johannine epistles were probably addressed to the same churches in the region of Ephesus where Timothy was serving and where the apostle John had last ministered before being banished to the island of Patmos. It should come as no surprise, then, that both 2 Timothy and 1 John would contain references to a mixture of true, born-again believers and those whose faith was outward only. Here is how John describes the situation in his first epistle: "They went out from us, but they were not of us; for if they had been of us, they would have continued with us. But they went out, that it might become plain that they all are not of us" (1 John 2:19).

The vessels of wood and clay who are given to dishonorable use (2 Tim 2:20) are likely similar to those who finally departed from the church, or who "went out from us" (1 John 2:19). The "us" from whom they walked away would be the vessels of gold and silver, which is to say, true believers in Jesus.

Although both groups publicly confess to serving the glory of God, not all do so in fact. The true believer, says Paul, "cleanses himself from what is dishonorable" (lit., from "these things"), by which Paul likely means they do not engage in the dishonorable behavior of the vessels of wood and clay. They are "set apart as holy" (lit., "sanctified" or "consecrated") by the Spirit and prove useful to the Lord Jesus. The good work of such vessels is honorable, bringing glory and praise to God.

REFLECT ON CHRIST

These two verses, together with what we saw in 2 Timothy 2:15, are a much needed reminder that not all professions of faith in Christ come from a truly born-again heart. In John 8:30 we are told that "many believed in" Jesus. Yet, these were the very people who were indifferent to Jesus's word (v. 37), who were seeking to kill him (v. 37), and were described by Jesus himself as children of the devil (v. 44) and liars (v. 55). These who "believed" actually picked up stones to stone him to death (v. 59). If there is any lingering doubt about their loyalties, consider the fact that they accused Jesus of being a Samaritan with a demon (v. 48; see also John 2:23–25).

To say that someone (be it a Phygelus, Hermogenes, Hymenaeus, Philetus, or a Judas Iscariot) may "believe" in Jesus but not be saved may strike you as odd. But much "belief" or "faith" falls short of saving efficacy. It is not the sort of belief that entrusts itself to Jesus and loves Jesus and treasures him above all earthly gain. "If you abide in my word," said Jesus, "you are truly my disciples" (John 8:31). The mark of true, saving faith, the mark of a genuine disciple (a gold and silver vessel) is abiding in the word of Jesus.

APPLY GOD'S WORD

How, then, do we know if we truly trust and love Jesus? What does a vessel for honorable use look like? We find several answers in what Jesus said in John 8.

First, the genuine Christian abides in the teachings of Jesus: "If you abide in my word [unlike those who 'swerved from the truth'], you are truly my disciples" (John 8:31). Second, the

Christian is free from the enslaving power of sin (8:33–36). This doesn't mean the true believer is sinless, but it does mean they should sin less.

Third, the Christian has God as Father and reflects his character in their behavior (8:39–44). If you were truly the spiritual offspring of Abraham, said Jesus, "you would be doing the works Abraham did" (8:39).

Fourth, the Christian hears the words of God: "Whoever is of God hears the words of God" (8:47). That doesn't mean we always fully grasp what is said in Scripture, but it means that our deepest desire is to obey whatever we do understand. Finally, the Christian loves the Lord Jesus Christ: "If God were your Father, you would love me" (8:42).

PRAY

O great Triune God, how I long to honor you with my life, my words, and with works that are empowered by your grace and are useful in the building of your kingdom. Set me apart for this purpose. May I always be a vessel of honor that brings glory to your name alone. Amen.

STUDY IT FURTHER

1. Read 1 John 2:3–6, 11; 3:6–10; 4:1–6, 8, 20–21. If, as Paul says, there will always be in the church a mixture of both true born-again believers and those who only profess to know Christ, what do these verses in 1 John tell us about how we might know the difference between them?

2. If we have already been cleansed by the blood of Jesus (see 1 John 1:7–9), what does Paul mean here when he speaks of true believers cleansing themselves from what is dishonorable?

3. How do we avoid crossing a line from being "ready for every good work" into a belief that somehow our good works are the basis for our acceptance with God?

Day 19

2 Timothy 2:22–26

READ

So flee youthful passions and pursue righteousness, faith, love, and peace, along with those who call on the Lord from a pure heart. Have nothing to do with foolish, ignorant controversies; you know that they breed quarrels. And the Lord's servant must not be quarrelsome but kind to everyone, able to teach, patiently enduring evil, correcting his opponents with gentleness. God may perhaps grant them repentance leading to a knowledge of the truth, and they may come to their senses and escape from the snare of the devil, after being captured by him to do his will.

MEDITATE

We begin this meditation by noting three emphases. There is, first, an appeal for personal purity in verse 22. In verses 20–21, we saw a call to avoid defilement from without. Here in verse 22, he exhorts Timothy to avoid defilement from within. He specifically mentions "youthful passions." Second, there follows in verse 23 an appeal to reject foolish and speculative arguments.

This exhortation is quite similar to the one we saw in verses 14–18, so no further comment will be needed here. Third, in verses 24–26, Paul provides guidance to Timothy as to how he must deal with those who err and oppose the truth.

Paul's appeal is both negative and positive: Timothy is to "flee" and "pursue," but with different goals in each case. Although the youthful passions he is to flee are inclusive of sexual sin, we must not limit them to it. Paul may have in mind selfish ambition, a craving for power, pride, shortness of temper, and other temptations that young leaders face. Like Joseph in the Old Testament, who fled from Potiphar's wife, Timothy is to turn and run away from all such passions. Both "flee" and "pursue" are in the present tense, pointing to an ongoing, persistent determination.

After his warning against getting involved in foolish speculations that serve no good end (v. 23), Paul advises Timothy on how to deal with hostile opposition (vv. 24–26). He speaks directly to Timothy's attitude and his aim. With regard to the former, Timothy must not be "quarrelsome," a verb related to the noun in verse 23 ("quarrels"). Simply put, he should avoid unproductive fights over secondary issues. He must also be kind or gentle to everyone. He is to be able to teach (a requirement for eldership in 1 Tim 3:2). He should be "patiently enduring evil" (one word in Greek, appearing only here in the New Testament), the antithesis of which is retaliation. Finally, he should correct his opponents with gentleness or humility—the point being that as gentle and humble and kind as he must be, he still has the responsibility to correct error and teach truth.

The repentance Timothy is hoping for is entirely a gift of God (see Acts 5:31; 11:18). Paul makes no guarantee but contends that God might, through Timothy, elicit a change of mind in his enemies and turn them from sin to a saving knowledge of the truth of the gospel. "Come to their senses" is the translation of one word that appears only here in the New Testament and literally means to sober up after intoxication. These enemies are portrayed as both inebriated and ensnared by the devil, in desperate need of deliverance from his will. There's no indication they were demon-possessed, but they were definitely subject to Satan's power and his destructive purposes for the church. One must acknowledge, however, that it is possible the final phrase, "to do his will," has reference to God's will, not Satan's, to which those delivered might then commit themselves.

REFLECT ON CHRIST

There is one phrase descriptive of faithful servants of the Lord that warrants our close attention. They are spoken of as "those who call on the Lord from a pure heart" (v. 22). This isn't something that one does in isolation from other devoted believers. It is *with* like-minded servants of the Lord. Together they "call on the Lord," by which Paul means they appeal to him, in faith, for forgiveness of sins and the gift of eternal life. This call is profoundly sincere and genuine, for it proceeds from a "pure heart" (v. 22b). The heart only becomes pure when it is cleansed by the blood of Christ shed on the cross (1 John 1:7–9) and washed through the regeneration and renewal of the Holy Spirit (Titus 3:5).

The challenge not to retaliate against one's enemies is massively difficult for every believer, Timothy included. The apostle Peter points us to the example of Christ himself who, "when he was reviled ... did not revile in return; when he suffered, he did not threaten, but continued entrusting himself to him who judges justly" (1 Pet 2:23). This is the posture in ministry to which Paul calls not only Timothy but us all.

APPLY GOD'S WORD

Knowing that repentance is a gift of God's grace, no less so than saving faith itself (Eph 2:8–9), yields several practical lessons. It instructs us about the sinful depravity of fallen humanity. Apart from God's gracious work, no one repents or seeks after God (Rom 3:10–18). It also delivers us from unbiblical dependence on technique in our evangelistic efforts. Moreover, knowing that both faith and repentance are the gifts of God guards us against arrogance and pride. It prevents us from thinking that we are ultimately responsible for the salvation of our souls or anyone else's (see 1 Cor 4:7).

This truth in 2 Timothy 2:25 ensures that God will get all the glory for the saving of a sinful soul. We can't claim responsibility for turning from sin to the Savior, which provides us with tremendous motivation and incentive to share the gospel freely without fear of failure. If the conversion of others were in our power to produce, who knows if we would see any success? This text reminds us that salvation is of the Lord, and that he will grant repentance to those on whom he has chosen to show mercy (Rom 9:18).

PRAY

Great God and Father, forgive me for thinking a soul's salvation status is somehow dependent on my eloquence or technique or persistence. I praise you in knowing that it is your sovereign mercy that grants faith and repentance to whom you will. Amen.

STUDY IT FURTHER

1. Read Luke 24:47 and Acts 2:38. We are commanded repeatedly in the New Testament to repent of our sins if we hope

to be saved. How do we reconcile this with Paul's statement that repentance is a gift of God that he "perhaps" will grant to some but not to others?

2. Read 1 Peter 2:11 where the apostle speaks of "the passions of the flesh" that wage war against our souls. Are these "passions" the same that Paul has in mind here in 2 Timothy 2:22? What specifically, of a practical nature, can one do to put such evil desires to death?

3. Paul is clear that pastoral interaction with those who oppose us should be characterized by kindness, patient endurance of evil, and gentleness. How do these exhortations address the problem we see today of pastoral bullies? In light of what Paul says, how might we identify bullies in the church and know the difference between them and those who are simply strong leaders?

Day 20

2 Timothy 3:1–9

READ

But understand this, that in the last days there will come times of difficulty. For people will be lovers of self, lovers of money, proud, arrogant, abusive, disobedient to their parents, ungrateful, unholy, heartless, unappeasable, slanderous, without self-control, brutal, not loving good, treacherous, reckless, swollen with conceit, lovers of pleasure rather than lovers of God, having the appearance of godliness, but denying its power. Avoid such people. For among them are those who creep into households and capture weak women, burdened with sins and led astray by various passions, always learning and never able to arrive at a knowledge of the truth. Just as Jannes and Jambres opposed Moses, so these men also oppose the truth, men corrupted in mind and disqualified regarding the faith. But they will not get very far, for their folly will be plain to all, as was that of those two men.

MEDITATE

The urgent opening to this paragraph (lit., "know this!") alerts us to Paul's warning for Timothy of perilous times about to descend on the church. This will transpire in "the last days" (v. 1). Some think this refers to the final days immediately preceding the second coming of Christ, but that would make it almost impossible for Paul's counsel to have any bearing on Timothy. Others contend the "last days" refers to the final years before the destruction of Jerusalem and its temple in AD 70. But the New Testament consistently uses this terminology to refer to the entire church age in which we live—the period spanning the two comings of Christ (see Acts 2:17; 1 Cor 10:11; Heb 1:2; 9:26; Jas 5:3; 1 Pet 1:20; 2 Pet 3:3; 1 John 2:18; Jude 18).

The "times of difficulty" relate directly to the moral degeneration of people, described by Paul in eighteen different, but related, ways. People will increasingly be "lovers of self" (i.e., self-centered); "lovers of money" (see Luke 16:14; 1 Tim 6:10); "proud" and "arrogant" should be taken as twin sins, both of which come from being a lover of oneself; "abusive" (lit., "blasphemers"; see Rom 1:30 where Paul speaks of those who are "haters of God"); "disobedient to their parents" (Rom 1:30); "ungrateful" (likely a way of describing an entitlement mentality in which everything is taken for granted); "unholy" (respecting nothing as sacred); "heartless" (i.e., devoid of natural affection, specifically in regard to one's immediate family); "unappeasable" (implacable; they refuse to make peace with their enemies); "slanderous" (from the Greek, *diabolos*, "devil," with the focus on constant accusation); "without self-control" (the antithesis of "self-control," which is a fruit of the Spirit; Gal 5:23); "brutal" and "not loving good" (i.e., disdainful of all virtue); "treacherous" (a word used of Judas Iscariot in Luke

6:16); “reckless,” “swollen with conceit,” and “lovers of pleasure rather than lovers of God.”

Paul then moves from their moral character to their religious hypocrisy. But note well: these aren’t overt pagans but professed adherents of Christianity. They retain all the external trappings of sincere believers (church attendance, prayer, knowledge of Scripture) but are devoid of the inner reality (see Matt 23:25–28). Avoid them! They are like a cancer to the body of Christ (see Rom 16:17). Worse still, they seek to entrap others in their wickedness by preying on weak, susceptible, guilt-ridden, untaught women, who are always hankering after something novel (2 Tim 3:6–7).

The apostle finds a parallel between such people and the court magicians of Pharoah. The one common link is their opposition to the truth, a theme that has appeared often in this epistle (1:8, 13–14; 2:2, 9–13, 15, 18, 25–26). The comparison with Jannes and Jambres suggests that these whom Paul has described also trafficked in false signs and wonders (see Matt 7:21–23; 24:24; 2 Thess 2:9). Such religious peddlers will eventually be exposed to the eye of the discerning believer. Be alert to them, but do not fear them.

REFLECT ON CHRIST

Jesus himself has provided us with a model for how to respond to such people. He was constantly opposed by those who put on a show of religious zeal but who were inwardly devoid of the transforming work of the Spirit. In one of the more terrifying passages in all of Scripture, he described them in this way: “You hypocrites! Well did Isaiah prophesy of you, when he said: ‘This people honors me with their lips, but their heart is far from me; in vain do they worship me, teaching as doctrines the commandments of men’ ” (Matt 15:7–9).

Neither Jesus nor Paul was afraid to call them out, and neither should we be. The danger is that they are often difficult to identify. Unless their behavior is openly scandalous, they join with God's people in worship and in honoring God (Matt 15:8–9). Notwithstanding the external example they seek to set, "their heart is far from" Jesus. They parade their alleged piety to draw attention to themselves and have no regard for the honor of Christ himself.

APPLY GOD'S WORD

There is an important lesson to learn in the way that Paul, the spiritual father, counsels Timothy, his spiritual son. While seizing every opportunity to encourage Timothy, Paul was not averse to speaking forthrightly to him about the enemies of the gospel and those who would attempt to undermine his ministry. In both instances, Paul is demonstrating what it means to display Christian love and leadership. We cannot avoid the conclusion that there are evil people, not simply in the world, but lingering in the limelight (and not merely in the shadows) of the church. Paul would fail in his paternal and pastoral responsibility toward his spiritual son if he did not alert him to the threat of false teachers.

It was, in fact, to the church elders in Ephesus, the city where Timothy was ministering, that Paul issued this warning: "I know that after my departure fierce wolves will come in among you, not sparing the flock, and from among your own selves will arise men speaking twisted things, to draw away the disciples after them" (Acts 20:29–30). We have just read of such "wolves" and the warning that Timothy, and we, must heed concerning their presence in the church.

PRAY

Father, give me discerning eyes! Grant me the Spirit of wisdom and revelation that I might know how to differentiate the true from the false and thereby guard your sheep from those who, in the guise of so-called godliness, seek to lead them astray. Amen.

STUDY IT FURTHER

1. What does Paul mean when he speaks of these individuals as having "the appearance of godliness" but denying its power? What sort of "appearance" is this? How might we be alerted to the presence of such people in the church? And what should be done about them?

2. Read Romans 3:10–18. As you compare that text with 2 Timothy 3:1–9, what do Paul's words tell you about the nature of mankind apart from God's grace? Are we by nature good and upright, or evil and unrighteous?

3. Is it possible to have a legitimate love for pleasure at the same time that we truly love God? Could it be that the answer is yes, if the pleasure we love is pleasure in God and all that he is for us in Christ Jesus?

Day 21

2 Timothy 3:10–13

READ

You, however, have followed my teaching, my conduct, my aim in life, my faith, my patience, my love, my steadfastness, my persecutions and sufferings that happened to me at Antioch, at Iconium, and at Lystra—which persecutions I endured; yet from them all the Lord rescued me. Indeed, all who desire to live a godly life in Christ Jesus will be persecuted, while evil people and impostors will go on from bad to worse, deceiving and being deceived.

MEDITATE

Paul's commendation of Timothy must have been a powerful encouragement in this young man's life. Although Paul would have been the first to point Timothy and all others to the example of Christ himself, he did not hesitate to encourage them to imitate his life to the extent that he imitated Christ. We see this repeatedly in Paul's epistles. "I urge you, then," he wrote to the Corinthians, "be imitators of me" (1 Cor 4:16; see also Phil 3:17; 4:9; 1 Thess 1:6; 2 Thess 3:9). This is not the counsel of a self-absorbed egomaniac, for Paul would have everyone do only what has already been seen in the life and ministry of Jesus.

Specifically, Paul lists several ways in which he has imitated Christ: in his teaching, his overall conduct, the very purpose or aim of his life (which, quite clearly, was to exalt and honor Jesus in every way), his faith, patience, love, and steadfastness. One might be tempted to push back against Paul when he commends Timothy for imitating the apostle in the way he has been persecuted and has suffered, but Paul is quick to remind Timothy of three things. First, he has "endured" persecution everywhere he encountered it (he specifically mentions Antioch, Iconium, and Lystra). This is Paul's way of saying that he did not back down or deny Jesus under threat of physical torture or loss of life. Second, in every case, "the Lord rescued" Paul. That will have held true until this final imprisonment that would end in his execution. But even then, as Paul will later say, "The Lord will rescue me from every evil deed and bring me safely into his heavenly kingdom" (2 Tim 4:18). This final "rescue" was Paul's deliverance into the eternal kingdom, where no persecution or suffering is found.

The third thing is not typically what Christians want to hear: "Indeed, all who desire to live a godly life in Christ Jesus will be persecuted" (2 Tim 3:11). Jesus himself assured his followers that if the world hated him, it would hate them (John 15:18, 20). To "live a godly life in Christ Jesus" is to believe what he believed and to make it known. It is to follow his example of purity, humility, and a refusal to conform one's conduct to the ways of the world. It is to prefer rejection with Christ over against acceptance by the rich and powerful. Such conduct will almost invariably provoke opposition, ostracism, and ridicule.

In spite of the believer's determination to live a godly life, evil people and impostors will continue in their wicked ways, thinking themselves to be enlightened only to discover that they are deceiving others and being deceived themselves (2 Tim 3:13). Living in the truth and walking in the footsteps of Jesus is a costly endeavor but eternally rewarding.

REFLECT ON CHRIST

Paul is determined to remind his spiritual son that his identity as a child of God and disciple of Jesus does not insulate him from the hostility of these "evil people and impostors." The mature believer is the one who embraces the reality of what it means to be a follower of Jesus in a world that hated and despised him. It means that we will be hated and despised as well (John 15:18–20; 16:2).

Paul alerted Timothy to this reality for the same reason Jesus did: "I have said all these things to you to keep you from falling away" (John 16:1). Jesus knew, as did Paul, that the greatest threat to our belief in him and our confidence in the goodness and greatness of God is suffering. He knows that if anything might tempt us to quit our faith and walk away and join the world in its ways, it is the reality of pain, suffering, loss, mistreatment, heartache, financial stress, and a host of other devastating and painful experiences that we encounter in the world. He knows that if we are going to remain steadfast and faithful and committed, we need to be informed and equipped about what happens to people who identify with Jesus. But with this warning comes the reassuring promise that the Lord will bring us safely "into his heavenly kingdom" (2 Tim 4:18).

APPLY GOD'S WORD

But why should the world hate Christians? On what grounds will they justify their persecution of the followers of Jesus? This question must be answered theologically. It ultimately doesn't matter what Paul, Timothy, or you and I may do. It ultimately doesn't matter how much we may give or how sacrificially we may serve or how compassionately we may love. The answer to the question is that people hate God. They only hate you because you love the one whom they hate. This is why we should expect persecution and suffering. The followers of Jesus will have the same effect on the world of rebellious unbelievers as Jesus did. We will seem to be out of step with the trajectory of society. We will appear to be on the wrong side of history. We will refuse to embrace the changing ethics of our day. If believers are in union with Christ and devote all their allegiance to the one to whom all loyalty and worship are due, the world of rebels will not respond with kindness.

The good news is that we can face this outcome with the promise of God that no amount of tribulation or distress or persecution or famine or nakedness or danger or sword can ever separate us from the love of God in Christ Jesus (Rom 8:35).

PRAY

Lord Jesus Christ, deepen and intensify my desire to live a godly life in imitation of your own. And as you do so, prepare my heart to be mistreated and hated as you were. Keep me ever mindful that no amount of hardship or heartache can diminish your love for me or jeopardize my eternal destiny in your presence. Amen.

STUDY IT FURTHER

1. If all Christians will invariably suffer persecution, what might we conclude about ourselves or others who seem to live carefree and insulated earthly existences? Does

this mean that we are not, in fact, living "a godly life in Christ Jesus"?

2. Does Paul intend to say that if we are persecuted, the Lord will deliver us from it ever happening again? What does he mean when he testifies that "the Lord rescued" him? After all, he is writing this from a prison cell where he will be kept until beheaded.

3. Paul appears to suggest that once evil people commit themselves to a life of wickedness, they will steadily degenerate from bad to worse and will even become more deceived than they were at the start. How does this affect the way you interact with stubborn, defiant, recalcitrant unbelievers? Is there no hope for them at all? If there is hope, how might you communicate this to them?

Day 22

2 Timothy 3:14–17

READ

But as for you, continue in what you have learned and have firmly believed, knowing from whom you learned it and how from childhood you have been acquainted with the sacred writings, which are able to make you wise for salvation through faith in Christ Jesus. All Scripture is breathed out by God and profitable for teaching, for reproof, for correction, and for training in righteousness, that the man of God may be complete, equipped for every good work.

MEDITATE

Our focus here is on verses 16–17, as they contain one of the more important statements concerning the nature, authority, and sufficiency of the Scriptures. Several observations are in order. First, should we translate the opening words of verse 16 as "all Scripture" or "every Scripture"? The word "all" has a collective sense and means the whole of Scripture, the entirety of the Bible, inclusive of all its parts. The word "every" has a distributive sense and means each Scripture individually—the various parts of the Bible of which the whole is comprised.

Whether it be "all" Scripture or "every" Scripture, Paul is saying that whatever is Scripture is God-breathed.

Second, back in verse 15, the words "sacred writings" refer to the Old Testament. On what grounds, then, do we extend the affirmation of inspiration to the New Testament writings? Peter refers to Paul's writings as Scripture in 2 Peter 3:14–16. Paul directed that his epistles be read publicly for instruction in the church, presumably along with the Old Testament (Col 4:16; 1 Thess 5:27). Paul called his message "the word of God" in 1 Thessalonians 2:13, and in 1 Corinthians 2:13, he refers to what God has revealed to him as "words not taught by human wisdom but taught by the Spirit." Finally, in 1 Timothy 5:18 Paul indicates that there is more to Scripture than the Old Testament. He places Luke's Gospel (or at least the materials from which Luke's Gospel was to be composed) on par with Deuteronomy.

Third, should we translate Paul's words as "all God-breathed Scripture is also profitable" (or "all Scripture which is God-breathed is also profitable"), or "all Scripture is God-breathed and profitable"? The former might (but need not) suggest that only some of Scripture is God-breathed, not all, and hence only some Scripture is profitable. The latter, however, is more likely, as most grammarians point out that when two predicate adjectives ("God-breathed" and "profitable") follow the subject and are connected by "and" (*kai*), they should be treated in the same way. It is because all Scriptures comes from God that it is profitable for the believer.

The meaning of "breathed out by God" (lit., *theopneustos*) is critical. The word "inspiration" can be misleading, for it might suggest to some an already existent text into which God breathed or to which he imparted some special spiritual or divine quality. The word means "breathed out from/by God," not "breathed into by God." The Scriptures are a product of the divine breath. The Scriptures find their origin in God, not in the creative genius of humans. In the Old Testament, the "breath" of God is his creative power (see Job 32:8; 33:4; 34:14; see also Gen 2:7; Ps 33:6).

Lastly, we find in these verses support for the doctrine of biblical inerrancy. The Bible makes no distinction between inspired and uninspired texts or topics, nor does it place any restrictions on the kinds of subjects on which it speaks truthfully. Some prefer the word "infallibility" to describe Scripture, the quality of neither deceiving nor being deceived. Others favor "inerrancy" or freedom from error. In either case, this means that Scripture does not affirm anything contrary to fact. Together, these two words express the idea that all Scripture comes to us as the very words of God and is thus reliable, true, and free of error.

REFLECT ON CHRIST

One of the reasons we embrace the inerrancy and infallibility of Scripture is because Jesus did. Being a disciple of Jesus entails not only doing what Jesus did but believing what Jesus believed. It is impossible to accept the authority of Christ without also accepting the authority of Scripture.

Consider the people and events of the Old Testament, for example, which Jesus frequently mentioned. He refers to Abel, Noah and the great flood, Abraham, Sodom and Gomorrah, Lot, Isaac and Jacob, the manna from heaven, the serpent in the desert, David eating the consecrated bread and his authorship of some of the psalms, Solomon, Elijah, Elisha, Zechariah, and more. In each case, he treats the Old Testament narratives as straightforward records of historical fact.

In referring to the Old Testament, Jesus declared that "Scripture cannot be broken" (John 10:35). Again, "It is easier for heaven and earth to disappear than for the least stroke of a pen to drop out of the Law" (Luke 16:17 NIV; see also Mark 7:6–13; Luke 16:29–31). He rebuked the Sadducees, saying, "You are in error because you do not know the Scriptures or the power of God" (Matt 22:29 NIV). When faced by Satan's temptations, it was to the truth and authority of the Old Testament that he appealed (Matt 4:4–10). Clearly, then, the question, "What do you think of the Bible?" reduces to the question, "What do you think of Christ?" To deny the authority of Scripture is to deny the lordship of Jesus.

APPLY GOD'S WORD

Why is it so important that we pay close heed to Paul's instruction in this passage? Several reasons come to mind. We should subject our souls to the infallibility and authority of the Scriptures and immerse our minds in its truths because the inerrant special revelation of God in Scripture has the power to change human lives and to transform the experience of the church. The word of God is the means or instrument by which the Holy Spirit regenerates the human heart. That is to say, the proclamation or communication of the word is the catalyst for the inception of spiritual life (see 2 Tim 3:15 where Paul asserts that Scripture is "able to make" us "wise for salvation"; see also 1 Pet 1:23–25).

Furthermore, the word of God is the power of God unto salvation (see Rom 1:16–17; 10:14–15; 1 Cor 1:18–25) and is the spring from which the waters of faith arise (Rom 10:17). It is from or through the Scriptures that the Spirit imparts perseverance and encouragement (Rom 15:4), as well as joy, peace, and hope (Rom 15:13). It is the word of God that yields the fruit of sanctification and holiness in daily life (1 Thess 2:13; 1 Tim 4:6; Heb 4:12; 1 Pet 2:2). And as Paul has said in our text, it is the God-given source of teaching, reproof, correction, and training in righteousness.

PRAY

God, I thank you for the Scriptures and the power of your life-changing presence that is mediated through them. Awaken me yet again to the beauty and immutable truth revealed in both the Old and New Testaments. Equip me, through the Scriptures, "for every good work," all to the glory of your great name. Amen.

STUDY IT FURTHER

1. J. I. Packer once said he finds it impossible to understand how error in Scripture can be profitable in any meaningful way. If this is true, what would you say to someone who denies biblical inerrancy and yet affirms that all Scripture is profitable for teaching, reproof, correction, and training in righteousness?

2. What does this passage tell us about the sufficiency of Scripture? What is meant by "sufficiency" in this sense?

3. Can you cite personal examples of ways in which Scripture has equipped you to live a righteous life—a life equipped for every good work?

Day 23

2 Timothy 4:1–5

READ

I charge you in the presence of God and of Christ Jesus, who is to judge the living and the dead, and by his appearing and his kingdom: preach the word; be ready in season and out of season; reprove, rebuke, and exhort, with complete patience and teaching. For the time is coming when people will not endure sound teaching, but having itching ears they will accumulate for themselves teachers to suit their own passions, and will turn away from listening to the truth and wander off into myths. As for you, always be sober-minded, endure suffering, do the work of an evangelist, fulfill your ministry.

MEDITATE

The connection between this paragraph and what immediately precedes in 2 Timothy 3:16–17 is obscured by the chapter division in our English Bibles. The Scriptures ("sacred writings") just mentioned are not to be hidden away or used merely as an object of study but must be proclaimed or heralded (*kērussō*, "preach," in v. 2) regardless of the time or circumstances. The words "in season and out of season" are not a justification for insensitivity to the audience, as if no consideration should be given to *their* circumstances. They apply to the proclaimer of God's word. We must always be prepared to proclaim the truth without regard to *our* circumstances.

Some distinguish between this heralding of the gospel and the teaching of sound doctrine. But given the repeated emphasis in 2 Timothy on the "sound words" (1:13), the "good deposit" (1:14), "the word of truth" (2:15, 18), and the "knowledge of the truth" (2:25; 3:7), which Paul calls on Timothy to guard and faithfully teach, the "word" in 4:2 must be inclusive of everything Timothy heard from Paul (1:13; 2:2). This is reinforced in verse 2 where Paul describes this preaching of the word as "teaching" and again in verse 3 where the preaching of the word is a countermeasure to the abandonment of "sound teaching."

The urgency of Paul's exhortation is reinforced both by his use of the verb best translated "solemnly urge" in verse 1, as well as his appeal to "the presence of God and of Christ Jesus." It is not only Paul's charge to Timothy but the latter's exercise of his ministry that are undertaken beneath the gaze of God and Christ. If that were not enough motivation, Paul reminds Timothy that Jesus, whose appearing (i.e., second coming) and kingdom are impending, will judge all mankind.

The importance of patient, faithful instruction through reproof (or awakening their conscience to sin), rebuke (or reprimand), and exhortation (or call to repentance) is due to the emergence of a time when people "will not endure sound teaching" ("for" in v. 3 grounds the exhortation in the perilous times that lay ahead). They will chafe when the truth is made known, preferring instead something new, different, and sensational that caters to their sinful passions. They will hanker after whatever doctrines appeal to them. Sadly, people won't want to be edified but entertained. They will not listen to the truth but will decide for themselves what they want to hear and then search out teachers who will oblige. They will consider the truth and pattern of sound words unappealing and will turn to embrace baseless myths (v. 4) and other philosophical speculations.

Timothy's response to these developments should be (1) to remain sober-minded or stable in times of instability (the present tense likely suggests perseverance); (2) to endure suffering (a repetition of what Paul has said before in 1:8; 2:3, 24; 3:10–11, 12); (3) to do the work of an evangelist (either Timothy had this spiritual gift or Paul expects every minister to be actively sharing the gospel); and (4) to fulfill his ministry, even when others choose to abandon their calling.

REFLECT ON CHRIST

There are some who argue that the reality of Christ's promised return is of little practical benefit. Such concepts, so they contend, serve only to fuel speculation as to when it will happen and to take our eyes off the pressing concerns of life and its challenges in the here and now. Paul would take great exception to this idea. His appeal to Timothy (and to us all) to remain faithful in the proclamation and instruction of the truth of God's word is rooted in the inescapable "appearing" of Jesus at the end of history.

This is consistent with what Paul and other New Testament authors say elsewhere. The sufferings we endure now are not worth comparing to the glory that is to be revealed to us when Christ returns (Rom 8:18). The reason we must "cast off the works of darkness and put on the armor of light" (Rom 13:12) is that the day of Christ's appearing is "nearer to us now than when we first believed" (Rom 13:11). The strength to press on toward the goal of our calling is found in our expectant waiting for the return of Christ from heaven (Phil 3:14, 20). Numerous other texts, in addition to this one in 2 Timothy 4, remind us of the practical, sanctifying influence of our hope in the return of Jesus Christ (e.g., Col 3:1–4; 1 Thess 1:9–10; 4:13–18; 5:9–11; 2 Thess 1:9–12; Titus 2:11–14).

APPLY GOD'S WORD

This text, though instructive to all Christians, is especially suited to faithful pastor-teachers who are called to preach and teach the whole counsel of God. This being the case, we must never lose sight of the fact that the stress is on the word "preach," or "proclaim" and "teaching" (vv. 2–3), together with the fact that people will cease "listening" to the truth (v. 4). The point is that it is not our responsibility merely to hear the word, nor even to stop after believing and obeying it, as if that would fulfill our ministry obligations. There is more to gospel ministry than guarding the good deposit from the deviation of false teachers. And yes, Paul is calling on Timothy to do more than suffer for the pattern of sound words entrusted to him. The urgent exhortation is to preach it to others. God has entrusted this treasure to us so that we might communicate it with patience and clarity to a lost and dying world. Followers of Jesus must hear the sound teaching that is found in the sacred writings of holy Scripture. Notwithstanding the immature demands of many to have their ears tickled, Scripture is for teaching and training in righteousness so that God's people might grow up in the fullness of Christ Jesus.

PRAY

My prayer, O Lord, is that you would alert me to the ever-growing threat of false doctrine and the tendency of so many to wander off into baseless and unedifying myths and doctrines of demons and of men. Keep my mind, heart, and ears attentive to your word and my feet firmly planted in the rich soil of biblical truth. Amen.

STUDY IT FURTHER

1. People don't like to think of Jesus Christ as the judge of all mankind. Yet here Paul says that he will judge the living and the dead. How does this truth about a future judgment affect the way you live in the present? Is it appropriate when sharing the gospel with an unbeliever to tell them of impending judgment? If yes, why? If not, why not?

2. Read Ephesians 4:11. Not everyone has the spiritual gift of evangelism, but all believers are called on to actively and regularly share the gospel with non-Christians. How seriously do you embrace this responsibility? What are some of the obstacles that prevent you from faithfully making known the good news of what God has done in and through Jesus Christ?

3. Can you cite some examples in the present day of false teachers who cater to the passions and whims of men and women? Why do you think their "myths" and other forms of deviant doctrine find such a receptive audience among some who profess to know Christ?

Day 24

2 Timothy 4:6–8

For I am already being poured out as a drink offering, and the time of my departure has come. I have fought the good fight, I have finished the race, I have kept the faith. Henceforth there is laid up for me the crown of righteousness, which the Lord, the righteous judge, will award to me on that day, and not only to me but also to all who have loved his appearing.

MEDITATE

Paul has a clear reason for his exhortation to young Timothy to be faithful in the proclamation and explanation of the truth of God's word. It is because he knows his time for this sort of ministry is coming to a close. In order to make his point, he employs two metaphors to describe his impending death.

First, he portrays his imminent death as if his life were a "drink offering" about to be poured out. Paul may well have in mind Numbers 15, which describes a drink offering of wine being poured out beside the altar whenever a lamb or other such animal was sacrificed. It is a vivid image of the gradual ebbing away of Paul's earthly life. The second metaphor is in his use of the word "departure" to describe his death. The word literally means a "loosing" and was often used of both a soldier striking his tent after a brief bivouac and the loosing of a boat from its moorings. The latter idea is most likely in mind here, as Paul envisions his death as the weighing of an anchor and the gentle drift of a boat to sea. He uses the same Greek verb in Philippians 1:23 to speak of his departure from this life into the presence of Christ ("my desire is to depart and be with Christ"). It is as if the desire to be in the immediate presence of his Lord pulls on Paul's heart like the waves and gentle breeze tug on the boat, seeking to detach it from the hold of the dock.

In three terse statements, Paul then sums up his life and ministry. It's important to note his use of the perfect tense in all three declarations. The perfect tense in Greek often speaks of a completed action in the past that has ongoing implications or results. Thus, Paul describes his life as a good (i.e., godly, Christ-exalting) fight that he has fought, a race that he has successfully run and won, and a faith that he has kept not only in the past but up through the present day.

All that awaits him in the future is the crown of righteousness that Jesus, the righteous judge, will award him on the final day (see Gal 5:5). Is this "righteousness" a life of holiness that Paul lived by the power of God's grace, or is it the "righteousness" of Christ himself imputed to him by faith? If the latter, we should translate this as "the crown which is righteousness." There may well be a contrast here between the sentence of condemnation from unrighteous Nero upon Paul and the glorious reversal when the righteous judge Jesus crowns his life and ministry.

The good news, of course, is that this is not a hope reserved solely for Paul or other apostles, but it is the confident expectation of all who "have loved" (once again, note his use of the perfect tense) the mere thought of Christ's return and our seeing him face-to-face (1 John 3:1–3).

REFLECT ON CHRIST

The "appearing" or personal, physical return of Christ Jesus to consummate his kingdom (what Paul here in verse 8 and again in Titus 2:13 will refer to as his "epiphany") is certainly the source of the apostle's resolve to fight, finish the course, and keep the faith. When we ask how a man such as Paul could endure the suffering that regularly came his way, the slander to which he was constantly exposed, and the opposition that daily threatened to undermine his work, the answer is his sincere and confident hope that Christ would return and reward the Spirit-empowered faithfulness of his servants.

But merely looking for or living with the moment-by-moment expectation of the second coming is not enough. Paul explicitly speaks of having *loved* his appearing. The love for the return of Christ is not so much a desire to be set free from hardship and physical pain as it is a deep and abiding affection for the person of Christ himself. Paul longs to see Jesus! His hope is fixed on being with his Lord and Savior, and it is this confident expectation that serves to sanctify Paul in the midst of his affliction while he remains alive on earth (see 1 John 3:1–3).

APPLY GOD'S WORD

This is a good time in our study of 2 Timothy to pause and ask ourselves, "Do we love the appearing of Christ Jesus? Are our hearts riveted on his return?" If the answer is yes, the question must still be asked, Why? What is it that we long for and love to see? Is it merely the promise that our bodies will be redeemed and glorified (Phil 3:20–21)? Do we love the appearing of Christ because then our enemies will be judged for their wickedness and their oppression of the church? Is our hope for life in the new heaven and new earth the driving force in this "love"?

All these things are entirely legitimate and will come to pass when Jesus appears in the clouds of heaven. But they pale in significance when compared to the prospect of seeing the splendor and beauty and majesty of Jesus himself. It is Christ first, and Christ finally, whom Paul loves to behold, whose glorious, transforming visage will make every sacrifice and all suffering more than worthwhile. Is this why you love the appearing of Jesus?

PRAY

I cry out to you, Jesus, majestic Lord and Savior, the righteous judge of all mankind, and say, together with Paul, "Our Lord, come!" (1 Cor 16:22). Bring your work to its consummate end and grant me the immeasurable privilege and treasure of beholding your face, now and forevermore! Amen.

STUDY IT FURTHER

1. Read Hebrews 2:14–15. Paul did not hesitate to contemplate his death and departure from this life, and he did so without the slightest hint of fear or apprehension. How do you deal with the inevitability of physical death? Are you spiritually and mentally prepared to stand in the presence of Christ Jesus?

2. Somewhat related to the previous question, if you live in fear of dying, why? What contributes to your anxiety about what happens the moment after you breathe your last breath? What has Christ done to relieve you of your dread of death?

3. Read 2 Corinthians 5:8–10. All Christians will stand before the Lord to be judged, not to determine their salvation but to be assessed for the deeds done in the body. How does this truth motivate you in the present day? Does it have any impact at all on how diligent you are, in the grace of God, to live in obedience to his commands?

Day 25

2 Timothy 4:9–15

READ

Do your best to come to me soon. For Demas, in love with this present world, has deserted me and gone to Thessalonica. Crescens has gone to Galatia, Titus to Dalmatia. Luke alone is with me. Get Mark and bring him with you, for he is very useful to me for ministry. Tychicus I have sent to Ephesus. When you come, bring the cloak that I left with Carpus at Troas, also the books, and above all the parchments. Alexander the coppersmith did me great harm; the Lord will repay him according to his deeds. Beware of him yourself, for he strongly opposed our message.

MEDITATE

Although Paul's primary desire was for the appearing of Christ (v. 8), he was exceedingly desperate for Timothy's arrival in Rome. Paul's urgent appeal for Timothy to come to Rome is coupled with the reasons why he needs him.

First, Demas had deserted Paul (the same Greek verb is used again in v. 16). This would have been especially painful to the apostle, as Demas at one time was one of his closer friends and coworkers (see Col 4:14 and Phlm 24). The reason may have been due to the oppressive conditions of Paul's second Roman imprisonment in contrast to the relatively comfortable incarceration of his first. Or perhaps Demas did not reckon with the demands that gospel ministry entailed. One thing is clear: Demas cared more for the comforts and ease the world offered him than he did for suffering for Christ's sake (see Prov 25:19). Was Demas a Christian who abandoned the faith? If so, we don't know if he ever repented. Or was he a false believer whose abandonment of Paul disclosed the true condition of his heart? We may never know.

Paul's desire for Timothy's presence was intensified by the departures of Crescens (v. 10), Titus (v. 10), and Tychicus (v. 12). There is no word of condemnation here, so we should assume they left or were sent by Paul on legitimate missionary outreach. At least Luke remained at Paul's side (v. 11). The request that Timothy bring Mark with him is highly instructive (v. 11). During Paul's second missionary journey, Mark had recoiled in fear, incurring Paul's anger and mistrust (Acts 13:13; 15:36–41). It may have been the encouragement from Barnabas, or the spiritual influence of Peter (1 Pet 5:13), or perhaps even the disciplinary action of Paul that accounts for Mark's restoration. It is a testimony to the grace of God that a man who had abandoned Paul out of fear is now regarded by the apostle as "very useful" to him "for ministry" (v. 11).

Verse 13 bears witness to the humanity of Scripture and Paul's authorship of this letter. The simple realism and down-to-earth request of this verse weighs heavily against any suggestion that a later imitator wrote the letter under Paul's name. Would a pseudonymous author have bothered to include such mundane details as these?

Paul issues one final warning to Timothy in verses 14–15. The "great harm" inflicted on Paul by Alexander may only be his opposition to Paul's gospel (v. 15b), but some believe Alexander was responsible for Paul's arrest and imprisonment, perhaps even serving as a witness for the prosecution. In any case, he is to be studiously avoided. "The Lord will repay him" may be optative, meaning, "May the Lord repay him." If so, this would be a wish or prayer by Paul, but it is more likely that this is a simple future tense forecast of what awaits Alexander. Paul is not vindictive, but he is assured that God will be just in his dealing with this traitor.

REFLECT ON CHRIST

The role of the Lord (most likely a reference to Christ) as righteous judge is one that we should not overlook. We are reminded of this in John 5, where Jesus himself declares that "the Father judges no one, but has given all judgment to the Son, that all may honor the Son, just as they honor the Father" (John 5:22–23). Jesus repeats this point a few verses later, saying that the Father "has given him [Jesus] authority to execute judgment, because he is the Son of Man" (John 5:27). Peter confirmed this in his message to Cornelius: "And he commanded us to preach to the people and to testify that he [Jesus] is the one appointed by God to be judge of the living and the dead" (Acts 10:42; see also 17:31).

In fact, even Christians will "appear before the judgment seat of Christ, so that each one may receive what is due for what he has done in the body, whether good or evil" (2 Cor 5:10). This is yet another witness to the fact that Christ is fully God, for judgment is a decidedly and uniquely divine prerogative everywhere in Scripture.

APPLY GOD'S WORD

We can learn much from the experience of Paul with both Demas and Mark. Demas at first gave every appearance of being a faithful, reliable, and devoted coworker with the apostle, but under the pressure of persecution, his true nature was disclosed. Mark, on the other hand, gave every appearance of being an unreliable, immature, and selfish pretender who was more concerned with his own safety than that of Paul's. But through the encouragement of Barnabas and the fatherly oversight of Peter, Mark demonstrated that he was truly born again and worthy of the trust that Paul would invest in him.

It is significant that Paul doesn't stop with affirming the sincerity of Mark's repentance or with his endorsement of Mark's return to ministry. Paul declares in no uncertain terms: "I need him! He is of great benefit to me in my ministry." The examples of Demas and Mark are a healthy reminder to us all to be slow to judge. We must be both patient and discerning.

One final observation concerns Paul's request that Timothy, "above all," bring with him "the parchments" (v. 13). Late in life, approaching death, Paul was ever the student of God's word! And so must we be.

PRAY

Gracious heavenly Father, keep me mindful each day that while others may abandon me, you never will. Never let me forget that I am not above the need for human friendship, companionship, and support. I give you thanks for all those whom you have graciously brought into my life. May I be as faithful to them as they are to me—indeed, more so! Amen.

STUDY IT FURTHER

1. Has there been a "Demas" in your life, a person you thought would never leave you or turn their back on the gospel? If so, how have you responded to them? If given the chance to speak to this individual, what would you say? How might you encourage them to return to the Lord?

2. Read Romans 12:17–21. Paul's instruction concerning how to respond to those who have done evil against us is to leave vengeance to God. Does Paul follow his own counsel when he declares (prays? hopes? believes?) that God will repay Alexander the coppersmith for the harm he inflicted? In other words, is Paul's statement in 2 Timothy 4:14 consistent with what he wrote in Romans 12?

3. As you think about the dispute between Paul and Barnabas concerning the suitability of Mark for ministry, have there been occasions in your life and ministry when a difficult decision had to be made about whether a person was trustworthy? On what basis did you make your decision? In making such a hard choice, did you remain open to the possibility of restoration? How might you have communicated that to the individual?

Day 26

2 Timothy 4:16–18

READ

At my first defense no one came to stand by me, but all deserted me. May it not be charged against them! But the Lord stood by me and strengthened me, so that through me the message might be fully proclaimed and all the Gentiles might hear it. So I was rescued from the lion's mouth. The Lord will rescue me from every evil deed and bring me safely into his heavenly kingdom. To him be the glory forever and ever. Amen.

MEDITATE

The "first defense" Paul refers to was likely not the trial proper but something along the lines of a preliminary hearing. That it was his first appearance suggests that there were more to follow. Thus, it may well be that Paul was so persuasive at this first hearing that an immediate verdict of guilty was delayed. We aren't told what precise charge was brought against Paul. It may have been sedition against the state. We do know that early Christians were accused of cannibalism (for eating the "blood and body" of Christ in the Eucharist) and incest (for expressing love for one another as "brothers" and "sisters" in the Lord).

It is difficult not to hear in Paul's words a deep sense of disappointment in having been abandoned by those whom he anticipated would be at his side. We don't know who these individuals were, but certainly it would not include those listed in verses 10b–13. They were probably sent by Paul as messengers or missionaries, and no negative word is connected to their absence in Rome. Those who deserted the apostle may well have fallen victim to fear, self-concern, or some weakness of character that prompted their decision. What is of special significance is that Paul prays (this is the force of the optative *logizomai*) that "it not be charged against them" (v. 16b; see Luke 23:34; Acts 7:60). This differs massively from his response to Alexander the coppersmith (v. 14). Alexander had spoken out of deliberate malice and opposition to Paul's message. These others, it would seem, failed Paul out of fear and self-preservation but did not deny the gospel itself. To them, he extends mercy and, in effect, asks God to forgive them.

Notwithstanding the departure of others, Paul stood firm, not due to his own personal resolve but because the Lord stood by him and strengthened him (v. 17). One thinks of the help or provision of the Spirit of Jesus Christ that sustained him during his first Roman imprisonment (Phil 1:19). The many gentiles who were able to hear the gospel from Paul were probably the crowds typically present at such imperial court proceedings.

The "lion's mouth" from which Paul was rescued would not be literal lions in the Roman amphitheater. As a Roman citizen, Paul would never have been subjected to that fate. Some think either Satan (1 Pet 5:8) or the emperor Nero is in view. More likely "the lion's mouth" was proverbial for any and all extreme dangers (see Pss 7:2; 22:21; 35:17). In this particular case, it probably refers to the judges who failed to reach a decision at his initial hearing, thus sparing him from immediate execution. The many evil deeds from which he will in the future be rescued is not his assurance of escaping physical death, as the alternative to it is entrance into the heavenly kingdom of Christ. No human verdict of guilty, no suffering in prison, no beheading will undermine the certainty of his eternal destiny.

Such a rock-solid promise to lay hold of amid intense hardship warrants a concluding doxology of praise: "To him be the glory forever and ever. Amen."

REFLECT ON CHRIST

The promise from Christ Jesus that he will never leave nor forsake his people is the central truth to which Paul clings in his final days of earthly life and ministry (Heb 13:5). As painful as it may be to have your companions leave you in the lurch when you most need them, you can always count on the sustaining presence of Jesus.

Paul never presumed that Jesus would deliver him from prison or ultimately from execution. But he knew that no manner or degree of persecution could separate him from the love of God in Christ (Rom 8:35–38). This reflects directly on the character and consistency of our Lord. Simply put, he can be trusted. And the Father has promised that since he has done the greater thing for us in the gift of his Son and the eternal life we have by faith in him, he will graciously give us all the lesser things that we need to remain faithful to him in the midst of trial (Rom 8:31–32).

APPLY GOD'S WORD

We hear much these days of people who have experienced abuse or some form of trauma from dysfunctional churches and misguided leaders. The pain that Christians suffer at the hands of other Christians can be especially intense and difficult to heal. To be mistreated by unbelievers is to be expected, but when those who are in leadership exploit their position of power and authority to do harm to the sheep, it is extraordinarily devastating, a heartbreaking betrayal from which many never recover.

Yet, if there was anyone who suffered at the hands of other Christians, it was Paul. Those who deserted him and left him standing alone weren't pagans. They were his fellow workers in gospel ministry, longtime friends, and traveling companions. Yet we see no bitterness in the man, no desire for revenge, no loss of love for them or for Christ. As much as it appears that Paul would have been justified in writing off the people of Christ as fickle and unfaithful, concerned solely with their own safety and personal welfare, he says it with unmistakable charity: "May it not be charged against them" (v. 16b). Let us learn from his example.

PRAY

Our great Triune God, I praise you and thank you that in spite of the disloyalty at times of your people, you remain steadfast in your commitment to us. I ask that, whatever the trial or oppressive circumstances in which we might find ourselves, Jesus would stand by us and strengthen us in our proclamation of his glorious gospel. Amen.

STUDY IT FURTHER

1. We often hear of people who turn away from Christ Jesus altogether because of the wounds inflicted on them by Christians in the local church. How would you address someone who tried to justify abandoning Christianity

altogether because of some injustice they suffered in the local church?

2. Read Romans 15:4–5. Paul says that God imparts endurance and encouragement through the Scriptures. Can you cite instances from your own experience where you sensed the Lord standing by you to strengthen you, by means of biblical truth, to press through some challenging circumstance?

3. What precisely is Christ's "heavenly kingdom"? How do we reconcile the focus on heaven in this passage with Revelation 21–22 where we read that we will spend eternity on a "new earth"?

Day 27

2 Timothy 4:19–22

READ

Greet Prisca and Aquila, and the household of Onesiphorus. Erastus remained at Corinth, and I left Trophimus, who was ill, at Miletus. Do your best to come before winter. Eubulus sends greetings to you, as do Pudens and Linus and Claudia and all the brothers. The Lord be with your spirit. Grace be with you.

MEDITATE

Of the nine individuals mentioned in his final greetings, three in particular are deserving of comment. Prisca (also known as Priscilla) and her husband, Aquila, are often mentioned in the New Testament. They were driven from Rome in AD 49 when Emperor Claudius expelled all the Jews from the city (Acts 18:1–2). They then traveled to Ephesus where they hosted a church in their house (Acts 18:26; 1 Cor 16:19). They evidently returned to live in Rome and once again hosted a church in their home (Rom 16:5a). In our passage, 2 Timothy 4:19, they finally settled in Ephesus. So, this couple lived in Rome, Corinth, Ephesus, Rome again, and then back in Ephesus. And everywhere they went they opened their home for the church—an incredible example of gospel hospitality for us to follow.

Priscilla was well-educated in the Scriptures and could articulate and teach biblical truth to others (Acts 18:24–26). Paul describes her, along with her husband, as a fellow worker in Christ Jesus (Rom 16:3). She and her husband also "risked their necks" to protect Paul (Rom 16:4). It comes as no surprise, then, that Paul would single them out for special greetings.

The Jews thought that Paul had defiled the temple by bringing Trophimus, a gentile, into its holy precincts (Acts 21:29). Of note here is not only that he was ill, but that Paul left him in this condition at Miletus. Contrary to what some have concluded, this does not mean healing gifts had been withdrawn from the church. Gifts of healing (1 Cor 12:9, 28) were never in the possession of a person to exercise when they might will. They were (and are) subject to God's sovereign good pleasure and timing. That Paul was still operating in this gifting toward the close of his ministry is evident from what happened on the island of Malta (see Acts 28:1–10).

Paul's change in prepositions from his opening salutation to this concluding greeting is of note. In 2 Timothy 1:2 he prays that grace, mercy, and peace would come *to* Timothy from God the Father and Christ Jesus (as reflected in Paul's use of the dative case). But here he prays that God's grace would go *with* Timothy. Grace, being the power of the Spirit's presence in and through us, first comes *to* us to encourage and sustain us, and then, as we close this letter and extend ourselves in ministry, goes *with* us to continue to strengthen and uphold us in the challenges we face each day. This is a consistent pattern in Paul's letters (see Rom 1:7 and 16:20; 1 Cor 1:3 and 16:23; 2 Cor 1:2 and 13:14; Gal 1:2 and 6:18; Eph 1:2 and 6:24; Phil 1:2 and 4:23; Col 1:2 and 4:18; 1 Thess 1:1

and 5:28; 2 Thess 1:2 and 3:18; 1 Tim 1:2 and 6:21; Titus 1:4 and 3:15; Phlm 3 and 25).

REFLECT ON CHRIST

The "Lord" whom Paul assures Timothy will be with his spirit is likely the Lord Jesus Christ. But what precisely does it mean that Christ will be with our "spirit"? When Jesus promised the disciples in the upper room that he would not leave them as orphans but "will come" to them (John 14:18), he probably had in mind the impending pouring out of the Spirit at Pentecost and the latter's permanent indwelling presence in and among the people of God.

Saying the Lord would be with our "spirit" (2 Tim 4:22; see also Gal 6:18; Phil 4:23; Phlm 25) does not mean the grace of the Spirit does not dwell in our bodies. By "spirit" Paul likely has in view the totality of our spiritual, emotional, and physical constitution. Should we ever grow weary, be it in our spirit, mind, soul, will, or body, we have the assurance that God's grace will always be with us.

APPLY GOD'S WORD

Christians are often heard complaining that they feel all alone, perhaps even abandoned by the Lord, in their time of greatest need. Nothing could be further from the truth. We may not always feel or sense the Lord's sustaining presence, but we must discipline our hearts to remain confident in believing that he is ever with us.

It is typically during times of severe physical suffering and pain that we allow ourselves to doubt whether God cares, whether God is even aware of our condition, whether God is still present with us to enable us to not lose hope. He is. The grace that comes *to* us when we immerse ourselves in his

Titus

Day 28

Titus 1:1–4

READ

Paul, a servant of God and an apostle of Jesus Christ, for the sake of the faith of God's elect and their knowledge of the truth, which accords with godliness, in hope of eternal life, which God, who never lies, promised before the ages began and at the proper time manifested in his word through the preaching with which I have been entrusted by the command of God our Savior; To Titus, my true child in a common faith: Grace and peace from God the Father and Christ Jesus our Savior.

MEDITATE

Titus, like Timothy, was one of Paul's spiritual sons ("my true child in a common faith"; v. 4). We know he was a gentile by birth (Gal 2:3) and that he became something of a test case for Paul's doctrine of justification by faith alone (with no additional requirements such as circumcision; see Gal 2:1–5). It is entirely possible that Paul led him to saving faith, but we can't be certain.

Paul makes it clear that he does not minister or write this epistle independently, but only as a servant (lit., "slave") of

God (although elsewhere he describes himself as a servant "of Christ"; see Rom 1:1; Phil 1:1). The translation, "for the sake of" God's elect (v. 1) reflects a preposition (*kata*) that typically means "according to" or "in conformity with." This has led some to interpret Paul as saying that he preaches in accordance with orthodox faith. But "faith" here is not the objective body of revealed truth that all Christians must believe. It is the personal, subjective confidence exercised by all who are among the elect of God. Thus, we should translate this as "for the sake of" or "in the interests of" or "with a view to promoting" the faith of God's chosen ones. The purpose of Paul's ministry, therefore, is to enhance and deepen the growth of each Christian's faith and dependence on God.

Paul also aims to expand the church's "knowledge of the truth" or understanding of God's saving purpose in Christ Jesus. The word for "knowledge" encompasses more than merely intellectual insight. Its focus is on the sort of comprehensive understanding that comes from experience. He employs the same preposition (*kata*) we just noted to make clear that this knowledge does not in any way minimize the importance of godly living nor is it contrary to godliness but serves instead to promote and direct it. Both Paul's ministry as an apostle and the faith of God's elect are grounded in the confident hope that eternal life is their promised inheritance. Contrary to those who suggest that a focus on the future is detrimental to fruitful living in the present, Paul contends that setting our hope on what awaits us is the very foundation for effectiveness in life and ministry now.

This hope is not wishful thinking but is rooted in the truthfulness of God himself. He never lies (see Heb 6:18) and would in no way deceive his elect children into putting their confidence in something that he then failed to provide. Like all of

God's saving purposes, this hope was ordained in eternity past (see Eph 1:4; 2 Tim 1:9) and only became known when it was faithfully manifested in gospel proclamation. All this came to pass in the precise and proper time that God determined.

Paul has repeatedly made clear that his preaching of the gospel was not by the commission or from the authority of other humans (see Gal 1:11–12) but solely by virtue of "the command of God our Savior" (Titus 1:3). He ministers under a divine mandate with which he has been entrusted. This serves yet again to confirm the unshakable foundation on which our faith and hope in the promises of God are based. Paul clearly wants all the elect to know with absolute assurance that God will fulfill his saving purposes for the elect in Christ Jesus.

REFLECT ON CHRIST

As was true in 2 Timothy, Paul places great emphasis on the nature and necessity of preaching the truth of God's saving purpose in Christ Jesus. We should never minimize the effectiveness of other means of communicating the gospel, but God is especially pleased to honor the good news when it is faithfully and truthfully preached. It is "the word of the cross" (1 Cor 1:18) that is the power of God for salvation. Indeed, "it pleased God through the folly of what we preach to save those who believe" (1 Cor 1:21).

The content of the gospel, when it is preached, is always Christ and him crucified and raised from the dead. As "an apostle of Jesus Christ" (v. 1) Paul has been commissioned to make him known. It isn't his personal testimony of what happened on the Damascus road or the impact of Christ on the environment that saves sinners. The gospel must always be Christocentric, making known what God has graciously done in and through the life, death, and resurrection of Jesus to grant the "hope of eternal life" (v. 2) to those who believe. Just as Paul was commanded to make this good news known, so are we.

APPLY GOD'S WORD

Divine election is a controversial subject. It has the potential to put Christians at each other's throats as each defends their understanding of this complex topic. But election is designed by God to serve as a foundation for our gratitude and an incentive to holiness in life. That is precisely why Paul mentions it here in the opening verses of Titus 1. He reminds us that his ministry as an apostle is for the sake of those whom God has sovereignly chosen to inherit eternal life.

This should be the motivation for all of us as we make use of our spiritual gifts and opportunities in the church to serve others. Our aim is to awaken the people of God to their identity as his elect sons and daughters and to promote the truth not only of this doctrine but of everything revealed for us in Scripture. Lest any of us ever think that God's sovereign election of otherwise hell-deserving sinners will undermine our commitment to godly living, Paul clearly says that divine election "accords with godliness" (v. 1). God's choice of each of us should empower obedience and sacrificial living to the glory of Christ Jesus and never become an excuse for licentious behavior.

PRAY

Father, I come to you with a heart filled with gratitude in light of your sovereign choice to set your saving love on my sinful soul. I deserved nothing but death and condemnation, but you chose to set me apart that I might receive the forgiveness of sins and the hope of eternal life. Thank you, Lord! May your Spirit awaken my heart to this marvelous, merciful, and altogether undeserved privilege that I might live in accord with godliness, always to the glory of your Son and my Savior, Jesus Christ. Amen.

STUDY IT FURTHER

1. What does Paul mean when he speaks of a "common faith" that he and Timothy share? How important is it that Christians in a local church share the same convictions concerning truth? What doctrines are essential and call for complete agreement among believers, and which ones are of secondary importance such that diversity of opinion may be allowed?

2. Does Paul mean to say that God does not lie or that he literally cannot lie? If the latter, does this place a limitation on God's power? What is the relationship between God's character and his conduct?

3. We live in a day when truth is widely regarded as relative and personal. Paul appears to speak of objective and transcendent truth—the knowledge of which is crucial to godly living. How do you conceive of the idea of "truth" and on what basis do you make your judgment?

Day 29

Titus 1:5–9

This is why I left you in Crete, so that you might put what remained into order, and appoint elders in every town as I directed you—if anyone is above reproach, the husband of one wife, and his children are believers and not open to the charge of debauchery or insubordination. For an overseer, as God's steward, must be above reproach. He must not be arrogant or quick-tempered or a drunkard or violent or greedy for gain, but hospitable, a lover of good, self-controlled, upright, holy, and disciplined. He must hold firm to the trustworthy word as taught, so that he may be able to give instruction in sound doctrine and also to rebuke those who contradict it.

MEDITATE

The charge issued to Titus from Paul is to establish order "in" (the preposition *kata* again, typically rendered "according to") the churches on the island of Crete. This is done, at least in part, by identifying qualified men who can serve as elders in each town. It would appear that no elders currently were in place, suggesting that the Cretan churches were quite young. The New Testament consistently teaches that all local churches are to be governed by a plurality of male elders. Crete is no exception (see Acts 11:29–30; 14:23; 15:1–6, 22–23; 16:4; 20:17; 21:17–18; 1 Tim 4:14; 5:17, 19; Jas 5:14; 1 Pet 5:1–5).

The English word "elder" is the translation of the Greek *presbuteros*, from which we get "presbyter" and "Presbyterian." Our English word "bishop" comes from the Greek *episkopos*, from which we get the word "episcopal" and "Episcopalian." These are two different words that describe the same office or authoritative function (see Acts 20:17, 28; Titus 1:5, 7). "Elder" focuses on the dignity and gravity of the person who serves while "bishop/overseer" focuses on the practical function of the office (lit., one who exercises oversight).

Aside from the requirement that he be able to teach sound doctrine (Titus 1:9), the rest of the New Testament makes it clear that these qualities are expected of all believers. There are sixteen of them. (1) He must be "above reproach" (repeated in v. 7); not sinless, but a man of such mature character that he gives no justifiable occasion for public accusation. (2) He must be, literally, a "one-woman man," by which Paul likely means he must not be flirtatious but faithful to his wife (see 1 Tim 3:2). (3) Whereas some believe his children must be born again, Paul more likely is saying that they should be trustworthy and obedient (the same word is rendered "faithful" in v. 8), specifically "not open to the charge of debauchery or insubordination" (v. 6). (4) As noted in verse 6, since an "overseer" is God's steward, or one entrusted with sacred responsibilities, he must be "above reproach." He must not be (5) "arrogant" or self-willed, always insistent that his view is the only right one, or (6) "quick-tempered" (an adjective related to the noun *orgē*, wrath), or (7) a "drunkard" (lit., addicted to wine; while total abstinence is not required, moderation certainly is), or (8) "violent" (not pugnacious or a bully), or (9) "greedy for gain" (he must not try to enrich himself by dishonest means; see 1 Tim 3:8; 6:9–10; 1 Pet 5:2).

He must be (10) "hospitable" (lit., a lover of strangers), (11) a "lover of good," (12) "self-controlled" or sensible (a word that will be used again in 2:2, 5, 6, 12), (13) "upright" (lit., "righteous"), (14) "holy" (better rendered, "devout" or "pious"), and (15) "disciplined" (virtually synonymous with "self-controlled" in v. 8a).

If an elder/overseer is to serve the local church well, he must (16) "hold firm" or be devoted to revealed truth with sufficient depth and accuracy that he can both explain and apply sound doctrine to the lives of God's people and expose and refute those who speak against or seek to contradict the word of God. Simply put, he must be biblically and theologically literate.

In sum, the office of elder is not for the fainthearted or weak. It is spiritually demanding, yet a noble task to which a man can aspire (1 Tim 3:1).

REFLECT ON CHRIST

Paul's concern for the local church is, not surprisingly, a reflection of his commitment to the glory and preeminence of Jesus Christ. The church is, after all, the bride of Christ (Eph 5:22–33) and should be honored as such. The purpose of the local church is to serve as a living gospel, a corporate testimony to the person and work of Christ in reconciling lost sinners to the Father. This alone justifies devoting considerable attention to the way the church is structured and the manner in which it carries out its gospel mandate.

In a related vein, the subject of ecclesiology (the doctrine of the church) is of vital importance. Simply put, bad ecclesiology hurts people. When the local church deviates from the principles of governance set forth in the New Testament (such as the one we are considering in Titus 1), it puts the spiritual welfare of God's people in jeopardy. Although there are rarely any guarantees, following the New Testament principles of local church organization and structure will go a long way in preventing the emergence of pastoral bullies and other forms of abusive leadership. Texts such as Titus 1 (and 1 Tim 3) are designed to provide inspired guidance for the way in which we "do church" and should not be dismissed as irrelevant to the spiritual health of God's people.

APPLY GOD'S WORD

We often hear people say things such as, "I love Jesus, but I hate the church." Our response to such a misguided declaration could be: "No, you don't love Jesus if you hate the church." As Paul made clear, "Christ loved the church and gave himself up for her, that he might sanctify her, having cleansed her by the washing of water with the word" (Eph 5:25–26). We must love what Jesus loves.

This is not to suggest that we should ignore the flaws of any particular local church. We know far too well the ways in which the church has failed its members and often inflicted deep and lingering wounds. But this should call us to a renewed effort to purify the church and to reform its structures and ministries. Believers cannot walk away from the church without walking away from its head, the Lord Jesus Christ. To love him is to love it. Our response to ecclesiological failures is not to jettison the church as a useless relic but to renew the church according to the principles and practices we see in the New Testament.

PRAY

Father, my heartfelt desire is that you awaken in me and renew deeply within my heart a commitment to the life and ministry of the local church. I am not blind to its failures, but

I see even more clearly in your word the depths of your love for the local expression of the body of Christ. Help me to see and embrace the affection in your heart for the church and reproduce this in my own, all to the glory of your Son. Amen.

STUDY IT FURTHER

1. Many churches have only one elder, the senior pastor, who operates as the executive leader of a congregation. How would Paul respond to this? Does it matter whether a church is governed by a plurality of qualified men rather than by only one? If so, why?

2. Some would argue that to be "the husband of one wife" means a divorced man can never be an elder. Read 1 Timothy 5:9. How does this text help us understand what Paul is saying about any man who might aspire to the office of elder?

3. Why is it important for an elder in the local church to be deeply rooted in theology and able to refute those who would deviate from the truth? Answer this question in light of what Paul says in Acts 20:28–30.

Day 30

Titus 1:10–16

READ

For there are many who are insubordinate, empty talkers and deceivers, especially those of the circumcision party. They must be silenced, since they are upsetting whole families by teaching for shameful gain what they ought not to teach. One of the Cretans, a prophet of their own, said, "Cretans are always liars, evil beasts, lazy gluttons." This testimony is true. Therefore rebuke them sharply, that they may be sound in the faith, not devoting themselves to Jewish myths and the commands of people who turn away from the truth. To the pure, all things are pure, but to the defiled and unbelieving, nothing is pure; but both their minds and their consciences are defiled. They profess to know God, but they deny him by their works. They are detestable, disobedient, unfit for any good work.

MEDITATE

Some may think that the robust requirements for an elder in the local church are unnecessary. Why must an elder be godly, faithful, self-controlled, and biblically well-grounded? Paul immediately gives the answer in verses 10–16. It is because ("for") there are many insubordinate, self-seeking deceivers in the church who, if not identified and rebuked, will wreak spiritual havoc among the people of God.

Paul goes to great lengths to describe the characteristics of those who are a threat to the integrity and spiritual vitality of the church. They are "insubordinate" (v. 10) or rebellious, always in defiance of the authority and leadership of the elders (this is the very thing an overseer's children must not be; see v. 6). They are "empty talkers and deceivers" (v. 10), perhaps even eloquent but making use of verbal skills to lead people astray. Those from "the circumcision party" (v. 10) is a reference to the Jews who likely were insisting on circumcision as a requirement for salvation (and perhaps Sabbath observance and Jewish dietary laws as well). They must be "silenced" or muzzled. Paul will elaborate on this in Titus 3:10, where he says that after warning them twice, Titus must "have nothing more to do" with them.

With monetary gain as their motive (what Paul calls "shameful gain"), they teach false doctrine that serves only to disrupt and ruin entire families. Even one of their own, a Cretan prophet (most likely Epimenides), rightly described Cretans as being generally "liars, evil beasts [i.e., irrational animals], lazy gluttons" (v. 12). As challenging as it is for us to believe that people like this can infiltrate the local church, it is true, and our response must be immediate and severe. Such people must be openly rebuked. This is not unloving, as the aim of such rebuke is to restore them to a healthy, biblical faith (v. 13; see v. 9).

The erroneous teaching is described as "Jewish myths" and "the commands of people" (v. 14). The former likely refers to extrabiblical legends concerning Jewish ancestors (see 3:9), while the latter would be similar to what Paul described in

Colossians 2:21–22 and again in 1 Timothy 4:1–5, namely, the prohibition of marriage and abstinence from certain foods (among other things). Such are the rules and regulations of men and not the truth that God has revealed.

"To the pure, all things are pure" (v. 15) is something of a proverbial statement (see Matt 15:11, 15–20; esp., Rom 14:14, 20). The "pure" are those purified or cleansed by the blood of Christ who are free to enjoy all of God's good gifts. The "defiled and unbelieving" refers to those who are not justified and forgiven and put to evil use those things which God has approved.

They claim to know God (v. 16). They are loud and insistent in their declarations of faith, but their evil deeds reveal their true spiritual condition. Their disobedience is in itself a denial of the very God whom they profess to know and serve. While the elect of God are "created in Christ Jesus for good works" (Eph 2:10a), these detestable people are "unfit" or unqualified for such acts of faithful obedience. Here we see, yet again, the way in which works testify either to the authenticity or illegitimacy of faith.

REFLECT ON CHRIST

The concluding verse of this paragraph calls for a more extended comment. At the heart of biblical Christianity is the close connection between genuine saving faith in Christ Jesus and a life of obedient righteousness. The Protestant Reformers were often heard to say, "Faith alone justifies, but not the faith that is alone." Paul is adamant that salvation is by faith alone, apart from works (see Rom 3:20, 28; 4:3–5; 5:1; Eph 2:8–10, etc.). This salvation, or being justified in the sight of God, does not preclude works but serves to produce them. The sort of good works that Paul envisions are not the root or ground of our salvation, but its fruit and the evidence thereof.

So, how should we respond to someone who professes "to know God" and to trust in Christ but whose life is a contradiction of all that God has called us to be and to do? A good place to begin is with a reminder to them of Titus 2:11–14 where Paul will make it clear that the very purpose for which God sent Christ to die was "to redeem" us from lawlessness and disobedience and "purify for himself" men and women "who are zealous for good works" (v. 14).

APPLY GOD'S WORD

For us to read of the vices that God condemns is good, but not enough. We must seek, by the power of the Holy Spirit, to cultivate the virtues that are especially pleasing to him. Instead of insubordination, there should be submissive obedience. In the place of empty talk and deception there should be edifying, Christ-exalting speech. Rather than teaching things that upset families, we must engender stability, doing it all without thought of monetary reward. We must not be liars but tellers of truth, not evil beasts who devour the people of God but gentle and tender in dealing with God's sheep. Hard-working and devoted servants of Christ must take the place of lazy, self-indulgent gluttons.

Our deeds must be of such a quality that they bear witness to the authenticity of our profession of having believed in God and trusted Christ for salvation. God desires that we be ethically attractive, not detestable or offensive, obedient to all that God has revealed to us in Scripture and never defiant of his word. We must be useful for every good work that God has foreordained for us (Eph 2:10).

PRAY

Father, I desperately need wisdom from you that I may identify those whose aim is solely to disrupt and destroy the harmony and holiness of the church. Help me not to be overly censorious but rather discerning of error and a lover of the truth. Let me not be naïve with regard to those who seek to bring ruin to the body of Christ. Grant me insight and courage that I might be sound in faith and stand firmly for holiness of life, all to the praise and honor of Jesus. Amen.

STUDY IT FURTHER

1. Read Romans 16:17–18. Compare the characteristics of false teachers in that passage with those Paul describes here in Titus. What do they have in common? How might you recognize such individuals in the church?

2. Some think that to rebuke another person sharply is unkind and unloving and that we should simply live and let live. Why would this be disastrous for the spiritual health of a local church? What are some of the issues that might call for a sharp rebuke?

3. Read Hebrews 9:14. What does it mean to have a "defiled conscience" and what hope does the gospel bring us to be cleansed of it?

Day 31

Titus 2:1–6

READ

But as for you, teach what accords with sound doctrine. Older men are to be sober-minded, dignified, self-controlled, sound in faith, in love, and in steadfastness. Older women likewise are to be reverent in behavior, not slanderers or slaves to much wine. They are to teach what is good, and so train the young women to love their husbands and children, to be self-controlled, pure, working at home, kind, and submissive to their own husbands, that the word of God may not be reviled. Likewise, urge the younger men to be self-controlled.

MEDITATE

Paul is clearly concerned with what we might call spiritual "good health." Four times in Titus he uses the verb *hugiainō,* translated "sound" (1:9, 13; 2:1, 2). Doctrine must be "sound" or healthy (1:9; 2:1), as must be "faith" (1:13; 2:2). There is a sense in which deviation from the truth is a life-threatening spiritual disease.

A great deal of what we find Paul telling Titus in chapter 2 either corresponds to, or is the antithesis of, those whom he denounces in chapter 1. Titus is to "teach what accords with sound doctrine" (2:1), the very thing Paul requires of elders in general (1:9). He must "exhort and rebuke" (2:15) those who "contradict" the truth of the gospel (1:9–10). His teaching must display "integrity and dignity" (2:7), as over against those who are "insubordinate" (1:10) and who ruin entire families (1:11). He is to make certain that the word of God is not "reviled" (2:5), in contrast with those who "turn away from the truth" (1:14). And he is to be a "model of good works" (2:7), unlike those who "deny" God by their evil deeds (1:16).

There are five classes or groups of believers that are the focus of Paul's exhortation and Titus's teaching: older men (2:2), older women (2:3), younger women (2:4–5), younger men (2:6), and bondservants (2:9–10). In 2:2, Paul speaks of older men (*presbutēs*), which is an issue of age, unlike the elder (*presbuteros*) of 1:5 which points to an ecclesiastical office. The virtues listed in verse 2 speak of moderation ("sober-minded"), the absence of frivolity ("dignified"), being sensible ("self-controlled"), and healthy ("sound") in personal faith, love, and steadfastness.

"Older women" (*presbutis*; feminine form of *presbutēs*) are to be "reverent" (honoring of what is sacred in their behavior) and not malicious gossips or accusers (*diabolos*), nor addicted or enslaved to wine (see 1:7). They are also responsible to "teach what is good" (*kalodidaskolos,* a word that appears only here in all of Greek literature; Paul likely coined it himself). Although the focus of their teaching is not explicitly restricted to younger women, it is implied. There are seven virtues to inculcate in the younger females: (1) love for their husbands and (2) their children; (3) self-control (a quality already noted for elders in 1:8 and elderly men in 2:2, also required of younger men in 2:6 and all Christians in 2:13); (4) purity; (5) diligent work at home; (6) kindness (or goodness); and (7) submission to their husbands.

It is unlikely that Paul is restricting all wives to the home, as if to say that work outside of it is always impermissible (see Prov 31; Acts 16:14; Rom 16:1–3, 6, 12). A godly wife can happily submit to her husband's leadership, provide a safe and nurturing home, and also generate income from routine labors. Paul's point, then, is not that a woman must stay at home and never do anything else, but while at home she should be diligent and industrious in caring for her family.

REFLECT ON CHRIST

Paul is clearly concerned that the word of God not be reviled through the disobedience or irreverent behavior not simply of the younger women but of all believers. The "word" here in 2:5 is both the gospel as well as the whole counsel of God, the "sound doctrine" and "truth" to which Paul has consistently called Titus to teach and defend. It is the believer's "knowledge of the truth" (1:1) that Paul, as an apostle, labors to articulate and uphold. And this "truth" or "word" (1:3) is primarily all that he preaches concerning what God has graciously accomplished for us in and through the life, death, and resurrection of Christ. If our "eternal life" (1:2) is dependent on our embrace of and trust in this truth, we can more readily understand why Paul insists on it being honored and not reviled.

This paragraph reminds us that the responsibility to teach and guard the truth of the gospel is not one that is borne only by apostles. Older men, older women, young women, and young men are tasked with the privilege of upholding the dignity and glory of all that God has revealed to us in and through his Son.

APPLY GOD'S WORD

People often mistakenly think that Christianity and its theological truths are meant only for intellectual speculation and debate. They struggle to see how the revelation of God in Scripture applies to the daily routines of life as well as the many relationships we sustain with others during the course of an average day. But Paul here clearly states that the sound doctrine and truth he so vigorously defends has massive implications for people of both genders and all ages.

It is precisely the sound doctrine that Titus is called on to teach that enables all believers to be sober-minded, self-controlled, and to live dignified lives of faith, love, and steadfastness. The principles that older women are to teach must likewise accord with sound doctrine. The purity of life and commitment to providing a stable and Christ-exalting home life that younger women are responsible to pursue are possible only to the extent that the word of God is the controlling and motivating force in their hearts. Is sound doctrine practical and achievable? Yes, by all means!

PRAY

Great God and heavenly Father, work in my heart by your Spirit so that in no way, shape, or form would your word be reviled as a result of my sinful behavior. May your word be magnified in and through everything I say and do. Make me quick to recognize the ways in which I bring reproach on the gospel and grant me mercy to repent and live in a manner worthy of the calling with which I have been called. Amen.

STUDY IT FURTHER

1. Is Paul talking about female elders in the local church in Titus 2:3–5? If not, how would you defend the notion that only qualified men can serve in this capacity?

2. Many Christians advocate for total abstinence when it comes to the consumption of alcoholic beverages. Do you agree with this? Paul says that the older women must not be "slaves to much wine." How does this statement address that question?

3. Read Ephesians 5:22–24 and Colossians 3:18. What does it mean when the New Testament says wives are to be "submissive" to their husbands? Also, what does it not mean?

Day 32

Titus 2:7–10

Show yourself in all respects to be a model of good works, and in your teaching show integrity, dignity, and sound speech that cannot be condemned, so that an opponent may be put to shame, having nothing evil to say about us. Bondservants are to be submissive to their own masters in everything; they are to be well-pleasing, not argumentative, not pilfering, but showing all good faith, so that in everything they may adorn the doctrine of God our Savior.

MEDITATE

Paul's continuing words of counsel in verses 7 and 8 are directed at Titus in particular. Again, in sharp contrast to those insubordinate individuals (liars, evil beasts, lazy gluttons) who deny God by their works and are "unfit for any good work" (1:16), Paul calls on Titus to be a "model" (lit., "type") of good works. Those who are elevated to positions of leadership in the local church are uniquely responsible to set an example for those who follow them. Paul specifically highlights the teaching ministry of Titus. His instruction is to be undertaken with integrity (2:7), by which Paul likely means accuracy and complete conformity with the revealed will of God. Dignity must also characterize Titus's manner of teaching, which is to say, he is to be serious and avoid flippancy. The manner of one's delivery must correspond to the gravity of the content. His speech is to be "sound" (lit., "above reproach," the same attribute twice required of elders in 1:6–7). Just as an elder must live in such a way that no justified accusation can be made against him, teachers of God's word must communicate truth that is not open to condemnation or contradiction. Paul specifically has in mind the possibility of evil things being said about "us" (2:8), that is, about himself and Titus and all who are responsible for public instruction.

Slavery in the period of the New Testament was rarely, if ever, grounded in one's ethnicity. People were enslaved as a result of war, or economic hardship in order to pay off indebtedness, or being born into it. Although slaves could be sold and had few rights or legal protections, many were well-treated, being provided with food, housing, clothing, and in some cases education. The New Testament never endorses slavery, but neither does it explicitly condemn it (although Paul comes close in Phlm 15–21; see also Eph 6:8–9; Col 3:25; 4:1; 1 Tim 6:1–2). Paul's primary concern is that rebellion or insolence among slaves might bring reproach on the gospel. His purpose, then, is not to endorse the institution but to regulate its practice. Thus, he encourages bondservants to be submissive, well-pleasing in their conduct, and to avoid argumentation. They should never steal from their masters but in every aspect of life "adorn" or clothe the truth about God in a way that corresponds to his glory and grace. As the beauty of a painting is enhanced by the frame in which it is encased, or as a jewel shines brighter in its setting, our behavior should reflect the splendor of the God who saves us no matter our earthly circumstances.

REFLECT ON CHRIST

If Jesus came to set free the captives, why wasn't slavery altogether abolished in the first century? As noted earlier, the institution of slavery is never endorsed by any New Testament author nor are believers ever exhorted to obtain slaves. Aside from the possible implications of Philemon 21, the New Testament never commands masters to free their servants, nor does it rebuke them for owning them. Neither does Paul command slaves to actively seek their freedom. However, in 1 Corinthians 7:21–22 we read this: "Were you a bondservant when called? Do not be concerned about it. (But if you can gain your freedom, avail yourself of the opportunity.) For he who was called in the Lord as a bondservant is a freedman of the Lord. Likewise, he who was free when called is a bondservant of Christ."

Paul and others undoubtedly wished to avoid the gospel being associated with social rebellion and the disruption of widely accepted structures in first-century society. Instead of engaging head-on with the institution of slavery, Paul chose to articulate ethical principles that innately undermined the ownership of slaves. His insistence on love and mutual acceptance in Christ for all, together with his doctrine of the spiritual and moral equality of both male and female, as well as both slave and free, in the sight of God (see Gal 3:28) undoubtedly contributed to the progressive abolition of the institution.

APPLY GOD'S WORD

Paul's reference to the ethical responsibilities of men and women, both young and old, as well as those whom he refers to as bondservants (*doulos,* often rendered "slave"), points us to the moral and spiritual dignity of all humanity. When it comes to our justification and acceptance by God, "there is neither

Jew nor Greek, there is neither slave nor free, there is no male and female" (Gal 3:28a). The reason is that all are created in the image of God, and all are "one in Christ Jesus" through faith alone (Gal 3:28b). No one in any category has an advantage over any other, as if God might grant preferential treatment based on gender or color of skin.

On the other hand, the distinctions in this text are not obliterated by the work of Christ. Each person retains their ethnic identity (be it Jewish or gentile). Men don't become women, or vice versa. And there still exists both those who are free and those who are bondservants. But they are all equally loved by God and must be loved by us and treated with equal dignity. It seems unavoidably the case, given the implications of this and other similar texts, that no form of enslavement can reasonably be defended or perpetuated in any society.

PRAY

Father, I ask that you would forgive me for any lingering tendency in my heart to regard a person of a different ethnicity or social standing as inferior or deserving of less dignity and honor. Help me to love and show the utmost respect to all as your image-bearers. Energize me to resist anything in my culture that would undermine the value of any man or woman, young or old, wealthy or poor, educated or not. Amen.

STUDY IT FURTHER

1. Although we are to teach in such a way that no one might speak evil of us, sometimes it happens anyway. How should we respond when someone vilifies our character and the content of what we say?

2. Some would argue that shame is never a good thing, but Paul says that by means of our sound speech our opponents "may be put to shame." What does he mean by this? In what way might their "shame" serve to awaken them to the error of their ways?

3. If bondservants, by their conduct, are to "adorn the doctrine of God our Savior," how might we do so as well? In what ways might our sinful conduct reflect badly on the Lord Jesus Christ?

Day 33

Titus 2:11–12

READ

For the grace of God has appeared, bringing salvation for all people, training us to renounce ungodliness and worldly passions, and to live self-controlled, upright, and godly lives in the present age …

MEDITATE

There are three words commonly used in the New Testament to describe the second coming of Jesus Christ. The term "parousia" (*parousia*) means arrival, presence, or coming (e.g., 1 Thess 3:13). The word "apocalypse" (*apocalypsis*) means revelation or disclosure or unveiling (e.g., 1 Cor 1:7; 2 Thess 1:6–7). The third word, "epiphany" (*epiphaneia*; or its verb form, *epiphainō*), refers to a manifestation or an appearing (1 Tim 6:14; 2 Tim 4:8; Titus 2:13). This third term tells us that when Christ returns in the clouds of heaven, he will not simply come but will be manifested. There will appear for all to see the magnificence, power, glory, and majesty of our Lord and Savior.

Of interest to us is that Paul also uses the verb *epiphainō* to describe our Lord's first coming. We saw this in 2 Timothy 1:10 and now again in Titus 2:11. Of course, in this latter text it is "the grace of God" that has undergone an epiphany, but only because the incarnation and death of Jesus were a manifestation of God's determination to graciously save sinners. Thus, if Christ's first coming was an epiphany of grace (2:11), his second coming will be an epiphany of glory (2:13).

Human sin and depravity are often portrayed in terms of darkness and blindness (see 2 Cor 4:4, 6; Eph 4:18; Acts 26:18). Much the same could be said of the original state of the universe, until by the word of the Lord, light burst forth. This is how Paul conceived of Christ's first coming. In that epiphany of divine grace, the saving power of Christ Jesus dispelled the darkness of guilt and condemnation. Salvation has appeared in the person of Jesus!

The translation of verse 11b is disputed. Is it that God's grace has appeared, "bringing salvation to all men," or grace has appeared "to all men, bringing salvation"? Some reject the latter on grounds that not all men have been exposed to saving grace. But if "all men" is read in light of 2:1–10, it would refer to all classes of humanity: older men and women, younger men and women, and bondservants, and not necessarily to all mankind universally.

But God's grace in Christ does not merely save, it also sanctifies. This grace does not merely secure our forgiveness but trains or instructs us, as would a professor in a classroom. It teaches, chastens, counsels, comforts, convicts, and empowers us to renounce (lit., "deny") ungodliness (or "impiety"), worldly passions (including, but not limited to, illicit sexual desires), and to live "self-controlled" (the same word already seen in 1:8; 2:2, 5, 6) lives of righteousness and godliness. To "renounce" or "deny" in this context does not refer to mere verbal repudiation but a moral renunciation that expresses itself in taking concrete steps to distance ourselves from sin experientially. In the light of this magnificent text, all forms of antinomianism and licentiousness are ruled out of order. God's saving grace gives us no excuse for remaining in sin.

REFLECT ON CHRIST

There is a sense in which Paul personifies God's grace in the person of Christ Jesus. In the first advent of our Lord, we see and receive the merciful kindness of God in saving us from a well-deserved death and condemnation. This is an echo of what John wrote in his gospel. The Word "became flesh and dwelt among us, and we have seen his glory [there is the element of epiphany], glory as of the only Son from the Father, full of grace and truth" (John 1:14). Because of the epiphany of the Son, from his "fullness we have all received, grace upon grace" (John 1:16).

God's saving grace is his free and unmerited favor by which he delivers us from a well-deserved condemnation. We must remember that this grace does not come merely to the *un*deserving but to the *ill*-deserving. It isn't so much that we don't deserve grace as it is that we *do* deserve hell. We aren't merely helpless apart from Christ; we are hostile to him and thus hopeless. We fail to fully understand what grace entails because instead of comparing ourselves with the infinite and perfect righteousness of God, from which we have fallen immeasurably short, we compare ourselves with one another. Grace is not God treating you less than you deserve nor treating you better than you deserve. Grace is when God treats you without the slightest regard for desert whatsoever. Grace is when God treats you simply and solely according to the infinite goodness and sovereign mercy in his heart. Neither human merit nor demerit factor in at all.

APPLY GOD'S WORD

The unbiblical notion that God's grace liberates us to live however we please has been a recurring and damaging heresy throughout the history of the Christian church. Paul vigorously denied this mistaken notion not only here in Titus 2 but in his letter to the Romans. When Paul said, "Where sin increased, grace abounded all the more" (Rom 5:20), some erroneously concluded from this truth that we should then "continue in sin that grace may abound" (Rom 6:1). By no means! For "how can we who died to sin still live in it?" (Rom 6:2). This antinomian (lit., against the law) deviation from biblical truth is what Jude had in mind when he referred to some "who pervert the grace of our God into sensuality" (Jude 4).

The apostle's energetic denial in Romans and his more positive explanation in Titus 2 are a clear and unmistakable reminder to us that God's grace does more than deliver us *from* something. It also delivers us over *to* something, namely, a godly, upright, and Christlike life as we await the second epiphany of Jesus at the close of history.

PRAY

O Father, keep me ever aware of my need of your grace to be justified. And keep me ever aware that this very grace is what secures my progressive, experiential transformation into the image of your Son and our Savior, Jesus Christ. May I, by your Spirit, never appeal to your grace to justify remaining in sin. Amen.

STUDY IT FURTHER

1. Read 2 Thessalonians 1:5–12. How would you respond to someone who points to verse 11 to justify their belief in the universal salvation of all people?

2. Some advocate for what is called "hyper-grace," the notion that any emphasis on the obedience of the Christian is to capitulate to a works-oriented approach to life. How does Paul's statement in these verses refute such an idea?

3. Paul has repeatedly emphasized the importance of us being self-controlled. What precisely does this mean?

Day 34

Titus 2:13–15

READ

... waiting for our blessed hope, the appearing of the glory of our great God and Savior Jesus Christ, who gave himself for us to redeem us from all lawlessness and to purify for himself a people for his own possession who are zealous for good works. Declare these things; exhort and rebuke with all authority. Let no one disregard you.

MEDITATE

Note the connection between verse 12 and verse 13. Waiting or looking for Christ (v. 13) is an activity that should characterize the life of an obedient Christian (v. 12) at every moment. This is not a passive mindset but an active expectation. It is not a fitful, momentary perspective, but a daily, never-ending, constant anticipation of heart and soul. Paul is calling on us to live consecrated lives while we wait for Christ's return. In other words, our waiting for the blessed hope of Christ's epiphany ("appearing") modifies or expands upon the sort of life that Paul has just called for in the preceding verses.

Although it is not evident from the English translation, there is just one article that governs both our "blessed hope" and the "appearing of the glory" of God. This indicates that these phrases are two ways of referring to the same event. Christ's return is a "blessed hope," because when he comes we will see him as he is and thereby be changed into his very image (see 1 John 3:1–3; Phil 3:20–21). It is also "blessed" because it will mark the termination of all sin and suffering and our entrance into the presence of our great Triune God, forever and ever.

There is one additional question in verse 13 that must be answered. Is Paul referring to the epiphany of two persons, God (the Father) and Christ, or only one? The latter is assuredly the case, as Jesus is himself our great God and Savior. Should anyone ask where in the New Testament Jesus is explicitly referred to as God, this text is certainly among those to which we would point (see also John 1:1; 20:28; Rom 9:5; 1 Cor 8:6; Phil 2:5–6; Heb 1:8; 2 Pet 1:1).

At his first epiphany, this great God and Savior voluntarily gave himself up as a propitiatory sacrifice in our place. He was neither coerced nor compelled but willingly yielded up his life to redeem us. Redemption alerts us to the fact that we were enslaved to our sin and that only a ransom could deliver us from it (see Matt 20:28; Eph 1:7). This act of offering himself as a ransom was substitutionary ("for us"; see 1 Pet 3:18). In this way God, through the blood of his Son, purchased us unto himself as "a people for his own possession" (Titus 2:14). Hence, "you are not your own, for you were bought with a price. So glorify God in your body" (1 Cor 6:19b–20). A "people for his own possession" (or a "special people") was often used to describe the nation Israel during the time of the old covenant. Paul's use of it here strongly suggests that he believes the church to be the new Israel (see Gal 6:16; 1 Pet 2:9–10).

We were not only redeemed but purified or cleansed from the stain of sin (1 John 1:7–9), a reference to both the notions of forgiveness and justification. The purpose was so that we would be "zealous for good works." We are therefore not only redeemed from death and condemnation but consecrated and set apart to live in such a way that Christ is glorified.

REFLECT ON CHRIST

Many today are mocking the notion of what is known as penal substitutionary atonement. Some even resort to denouncing it as a form of cosmic child abuse, as if God the Father were a celestial bully compelling his helpless Son to be punished for our sins. But Paul is quite clear, as was Jesus himself, that the Son "gave himself" as a joyful substitute in our stead, there to exhaust in himself the wrath that we so justly deserved. Jesus declared, "For this reason the Father loves me, because I lay down my life that I may take it up again. No one takes it from me, but I lay it down of my own accord. I have authority to lay it down, and I have authority to take it up again" (John 10:17–18). In this way, the Son offered himself as a propitiatory sacrifice, satisfying the righteous wrath and justice of God (Rom 3:25; 1 John 2:1–2; 4:10).

Apart from the righteous Son dying in the place of the unrighteous (1 Pet 3:18), placing himself in the position of acquiring our guilt (2 Cor 5:21), there is no gospel. The good news is that because of this atoning work on the cross there is now "for those who are in Christ Jesus" absolutely "no condemnation" (Rom 8:1).

APPLY GOD'S WORD

There are two deadly threats to Christ-exalting Christian living: legalism and licentiousness. The former demands that we meet certain conditions of obedience in order to have eternal life. The latter ignores the demands of God's law, insisting that since Christ obeyed it for us and died to endure its penalty, we are free to live in unrepentant sin. It is licentiousness that Paul refutes in our passage.

But to what kind of life are we called? For what purpose did the Son of God suffer and die? Paul referred to us in Titus 1:1 as God's "elect." But to what end have we been chosen? In addition to our text in Titus 2, Paul declares that we have been predestined "to be conformed to the image of his Son" (Rom 8:29). He "chose us" in Christ "that we should be holy and blameless before him" (Eph 1:4). We are God's "workmanship, created in Christ Jesus for good works, which God prepared beforehand, that we should walk in them" (Eph 2:10; also 2 Thess 2:13; 2 Tim 1:8b–9a; 1 Pet 1:1–2). Salvation cannot be severed from sanctification. The latter is the fruit of the former. The former is the root of the latter.

PRAY

Holy Spirit of God, I bring my heartfelt petition to you. Set me apart unto Christ Jesus. Work in me all that is pleasing to him. Make use of my thoughts, words, and life to honor the one who died to purify me for himself. May I never appeal to grace to rationalize a life of sinful license. Amen.

STUDY IT FURTHER

1. Paul not only describes Jesus Christ as our Savior but as our "great God." There is hardly a more explicit assertion of the true deity of Jesus to be found in the New Testament. Take a few minutes to read other passages that describe the godhood of Jesus: John 1:1; 5:18; 8:58; 10:30; 20:26–29; Romans 9:5; 1 Corinthians 8:6; Philippians 2:6–11; Colossians 1:15–20; Hebrews 1:8–9.

2. Read Romans 1:6. How does it affect your heart to hear that you are God's own possession? In contrast to those who live as if they belonged to no one, Christians can rest assured that they belong to the Lord.

3. Paul is concerned that some may disregard Titus because of his teaching of this gospel truth. Have you experienced this when you shared the gospel with someone? How should you respond to rejection and ridicule such as this?

Day 35

Titus 3:1–3

READ

Remind them to be submissive to rulers and authorities, to be obedient, to be ready for every good work, to speak evil of no one, to avoid quarreling, to be gentle, and to show perfect courtesy toward all people. For we ourselves were once foolish, disobedient, led astray, slaves to various passions and pleasures, passing our days in malice and envy, hated by others and hating one another.

MEDITATE

Lest one think that Paul was an arrogant, self-inflated, self-righteous man who took perverse joy in pointing out the sins of others, he reminds Titus and us of what our lives were like before we came to saving faith in Christ Jesus. In fact, the very basis ("for," v. 3) on which he issues yet another call for obedient, godly living is the undeniable, though painful, reality of what all of us once were (that is, prior to the experience of God's saving grace described in 2:11–15).

The people of Crete were notorious for their immodest, idolatrous, and insubordinate behavior. Paul's words in verses

1–2 suggest that even some in the Christian community were becoming disrespectful toward the governing authorities and slack in their obedience to Christ. The verb "remind" suggests that the believers in Crete already knew of their duty to the civil authorities. Paul wants them to be certain never to think that allegiance to Christ precludes the importance of submission to those whom God has placed in authority over us (see Rom 13:1–7; 1 Pet 2:13–17). There are, of course, limitations to the authority of earthly rulers. If they should ever command what God has forbidden or prohibit what God has commanded, the believer is responsible to the higher authority of inspired Scripture (see Acts 4:18–20; 5:27–32).

Paul's counsel in verse 2 is not designed to prohibit speaking out against immorality, nor does he wish us to condone the sinful ways of ungodly people. After all, the apostle himself has spoken quite explicitly and with considerable passion of the sins of unbelievers and our responsibility to rebuke them and call them to repentance (see Titus 1:10–16). There is nothing inconsistent in Paul prohibiting speaking evil of others (lit., blaspheming them) while at the same time identifying their sin. If they are truly guilty of transgressions, it is quite loving to call them to account for their behavior. It is entirely possible for Christians to avoid unnecessary arguments, to be "gentle" and "courteous" at the same time that we hold up the standard of righteousness that God has called us to embrace.

Paul's remedy for self-righteousness and high-minded denunciation of others is his reminder that before we came to know Christ, we were no different from them. Let us be quick to acknowledge that we too were "foolish" (devoid of spiritual understanding and ignorant of the gospel), "disobedient" (to God), "led astray" (into all manner of ungodly behavior), and "slaves" to any number of sinful "passions" and "pleasures" (*hēdonē*, from which we derive "hedonism"). Somewhat ironically, it is here, in their unbridled capitulation to every manner of lust, that unbelievers think themselves free.

We wasted our time by indulging ourselves in "malice" (more literally, "wickedness") and "envy." We were "hated by others" (because we were despicable, odious, repulsive, and disgusting) and "hated" them in return. We were deserving of others' hatred, and we were willing participants in it as well. Clearly, Paul was not one to whitewash his former life or that of Titus and the believing community in Crete.

REFLECT ON CHRIST

Paul reminds us to be "gentle" (*prautēs*), which recalls the one thing that Jesus said about himself: "Come to me, all who labor and are heavy laden, and I will give you rest. Take my yoke upon you, and learn from me, for I am gentle [*praus*] and lowly in heart, and you will find rest for your souls" (Matt 11:28–29). Jesus could have pointed to any number of his attributes and personal characteristics. We would hardly have given it a second thought had he described himself as powerful and authoritative, or perhaps holy and just, or even if he had pointed to his ability to drive out demons and heal the sick.

But our Lord wanted us to know that we can come to him without hesitation or fear, without the slightest concern that our weaknesses and failures might disqualify us from enjoying his presence. And to do this, he identifies himself as being "gentle and lowly." I can think of no greater incentive to run *to* Christ rather than *from* him, especially when we are burdened by our sins and shortcomings.

APPLY GOD'S WORD

Although it is undeniably painful to think back on our lives before faith in Christ, it can serve a good and godly purpose. If nothing else, it should stir within us a measure of compassion for those who are still enthralled with the world and enslaved to a variety of sinful desires. Moreover, it should awaken within our hearts a deeper and more intense feeling of gratitude, as we know the depths of human depravity from which Christ has so graciously delivered us.

At the same time, we should not wallow in the past or make too much of how sordid our behavior used to be. As Paul wrote to the church in Philippi, he is committed to "forgetting what lies behind and straining forward to what lies ahead" (Phil 3:13). Personal testimonies that rehash in graphic detail our former sins tend to bring more attention to ourselves than to the Savior who set us free and forgave us all our transgressions. We must keep in mind the words of the hymn, "Grace that is greater than all our sin,"[2] and labor to keep the focus on what Christ has done to save us above what we have done that made our salvation necessary in the first place.

PRAY

Father, I confess how prone I am to speak evil of others in order to justify my own sinful ways. I pray that you would curb my tongue and put a bridle on my mouth that I may not blaspheme or belittle others. Grant me discernment to know the difference between speaking truthfully of the wickedness of others

2. "Grace Greater Than Our Sin," *Baptist Hymnal* (Brentwood, TN: Lifeway, 2008), 105.

and speaking evil of them. Grant me the mind and heart of Jesus so that even when I speak of the sins of those who oppose you, I would do it in love for them and from concern for their eternal welfare. Amen.

STUDY IT FURTHER

1. How absolute is the command that we be "submissive" to the governing authorities? What circumstances in today's world might call for what is known as "civil disobedience"?

2. What does Paul mean when he calls us to show "perfect courtesy" to others? Is it possible to be firm and forthright in our defense of truth at the same time that we are courteous to those who disagree with us? Can you give examples of this from your own experience?

3. How helpful is it for us to reflect often on our immoral and ungodly conduct before we were saved? When is it a hindrance to future growth in Christ, and when might it be beneficial?

pollution of sin. The genitive ("of") in the phrase "renewal of the Holy Spirit" is obviously subjective. The Spirit doesn't need renewal! He is the source and cause of *our* renewal.

REFLECT ON CHRIST

As we will see in verse 6, the gift and saving work of the Holy Spirit is "through Jesus Christ our Savior." This prepositional phrase points to several important truths. First, John the Baptist prophesied that Jesus would baptize his followers "with the Holy Spirit and fire" (Matt 3:11). And Jesus himself promised that following his ascension and exaltation, he would "ask the Father" who will give us "another Helper, to be with you forever, even the Spirit of truth" (John 14:16–17). The Father will send us "the Helper, the Holy Spirit," in Christ's name (John 14:26; see also 15:26). Peter confirms this entire scenario in his sermon on the day of Pentecost. It is because Jesus has been "exalted at the right hand of God" that he "received from the Father the promise of the Holy Spirit" whom "he has poured out" on the believing company (Acts 2:33).

It is because of, or through, the person and work of Jesus in his life, death, and resurrection that we now have received and experience the fullness of the Spirit's activity in causing us to be born again and renewed spiritually unto faith in Christ.

APPLY GOD'S WORD

We who have come to believe the gospel do so only because there has taken place within us a radical and spiritually pervasive transformation in which our minds, souls, hearts—indeed, our entire personality—has been renewed by the Spirit of God. Some believe that regeneration or being born again is brought to pass by the divine will and human will working in conjunction.

Or, if God alone regenerates, he does so only when and because the individual believes by an act of free will.

But I believe Paul and other New Testament authors would insist that the sole cause of regeneration or being born again is the will of God (see John 1:12–13). God sovereignly and efficaciously regenerates, and as a consequence of his action, we move in response. Therefore, the individual is passive in regeneration, neither preparing himself nor making himself receptive to what God will do. Regeneration is a change wrought in us by God, not an autonomous act performed by us for ourselves. A person's status in regard to regeneration is that of a recipient, not a contributor.

Thus, in the experience of regeneration, beneath and before all positive human response to the gospel (whether faith, repentance, love, or conversion), there is a supernatural, efficacious, and altogether mysterious work of the Holy Spirit that is both prior to and the effectual cause of all activity on the part of the human. To sum up, the Holy Spirit regenerates a person in order that a person may convert to God.

PRAY

Praise be to you, O Lord, for your sovereign, saving mercy by which I have been renewed and brought to life by the work of your Spirit. Open my eyes yet again to the marvel of your mercy and the abundance of your saving grace, all of which is mine through the person and work of Jesus, my Savior. Amen.

STUDY IT FURTHER

1. Can you cite specific instances in the earthly life and ministry of Jesus when his kindness was uniquely on display?

Was he being kind when he rebuked the religious leaders in harsh terms? How do you reconcile these two realities?

2. Is Paul saying that baptism in water is necessary to be cleansed from the guilt of our sin? If not, what texts and arguments would you employ to refute such a notion?

3. In what ways are you experiencing the renewal of the Holy Spirit today? How has this ministry of the Spirit changed your life? What might you do to increase this ministry of renewal in your life?

Day 37

Titus 3:6–7

READ

... whom he poured out on us richly through Jesus Christ our Savior, so that being justified by his grace we might become heirs according to the hope of eternal life.

MEDITATE

The gift of the Holy Spirit is entirely the fruit of the work of Christ Jesus on the cross and his resurrection from the dead. This gift was not granted piecemeal or in measured portions, but "richly." God has lavished us with the Spirit. The imagery of the Spirit being "poured out" (and not merely "given") highlights the abundant, overflowing, effusive way in which the Spirit comes to the believer. This same imagery is found in Peter's description of the events on the day of Pentecost. Quoting Joel 2:28–32 he says that "in the last days it shall be, God declares, that I will pour out my Spirit on all flesh" (Acts 2:17). And again, "in those days I will pour out my Spirit, and they shall prophesy" (Acts 2:18). Paul alludes to this in Romans 5:5, reminding us that "hope does not put us to shame, because God's love has been poured into our hearts through the Holy Spirit who has been given to us."

The result of God's saving work through the Spirit is that we are "justified by his grace" (Titus 3:7). To be justified means that we are declared righteous, not made righteous. It is objective, not subjective, meaning, it is something done for us, not in us. It is a legal declaration of our standing before God, not an emotional release of guilt. Whereas we do not feel justification when it occurs, once we comprehend what God has done, there may be great exhilaration of soul and spirit.

Justification is both acquittal and acceptance. It involves both the forgiveness of sins and the receiving of the righteousness of Christ. God not only declares us "not guilty," he declares us "righteous." Mere pardon would leave us spiritually naked with no righteousness. Pardon might save us from hell, but it wouldn't get us into heaven. Justification is exclusive in the sense that there is no middle ground: you either are, or are not, justified. By extensive we mean that all sins are dealt with, whether past, present, or future.

Justification is both instantaneous and irreversible. It is a position or status to which we are elevated in the moment our verdict is announced. It is not a process. Furthermore, it cannot be lost. God's verdict will never be appealed to a higher court (see Rom 8:31–34). Justification is "by his grace" and is received by faith, being freely bestowed by God (see Rom 3:24; John 15:25). Thus, the sinner is justified *through faith on account of Christ*, rather than *on account of faith through Christ*. We are not justified because we believe. Faith is not a human work that merits justification. We are justified on account of, or because of, Christ, whose righteousness we receive passively, through faith, and in doing so are made heirs of eternal life.

REFLECT ON CHRIST

What is it, precisely, that we inherit when we are justified by the grace of Christ Jesus? There are numerous blessings that we might mention. Although justification is not identical with forgiveness of sins, when we experience the former, we obtain the latter. We are assured that when Christ returns our bodies will be transformed to be made like his own glorious body (Phil 3:20–21), never again to suffer from sin or disease or weakness. We are also promised life in the new heaven and new earth with all its attendant blessings (see Rev 21–22).

But the greatest and most glorious benefit of justification by grace in Christ alone is that we get God. The "washing of regeneration and renewal of the Holy Spirit" is wonderful not as an end in itself, but because it makes possible our unmediated experience of the beauty and majesty of God himself. Forgiveness, adoption, and reconciliation are likewise splendid gifts of God's kindness primarily because they prepare us to stand "blameless before the presence of his glory with great joy" (Jude 24). Getting God, seeing God, enjoying God, and being eternally satisfied with God are the ultimate goals of being justified by his grace.

APPLY GOD'S WORD

It is the hope of eternal life that sustains us in the midst of suffering and empowers us to press through whatever hardship and trial we may face. The hope that we have of entering fully and finally into the experience of eternal life is not wishful thinking. This hope that Paul has in view is neither tenuous nor conditional. It is rock solid and guaranteed. Biblical hope is far more than a passing desire that certain things will come to pass. The hope that is ours by virtue of being justified by the grace of Christ Jesus is the well-founded assurance, rooted in the promise of God himself, that what he has decreed will in fact be fulfilled. Paul opened this epistle by referring to the "hope of eternal life, which God, who never lies, promised before the ages began" (Titus 1:2). Our hope is founded on the unshakeable confidence that everything God has promised to do for us will be done. Our hope is warranted because God does not lie. This is why the author of Hebrews spoke of his desire that we would "show the same earnestness to have the full assurance of hope until the end" (Heb 6:11).

PRAY

Lord, I thank you that you do not lie. Indeed, you cannot lie. You always fulfill your promises to me. I ask that you would deepen and intensify this conviction in my heart that I may rest confidently in my hope for eternal life and in your presence that remains steadfast and sure. I give all praise to Jesus, our Savior, through whom all this has been made not only possible, but certain. Amen.

STUDY IT FURTHER

1. Both Roman Catholicism and Eastern Orthodoxy teach that justification is a process throughout the course of life that is increased in our hearts through works of obedience. Is this correct? If not, how would you refute it?

2. Read Romans 8:17. What does it mean to be an "heir" according to the hope of eternal life? What precisely is it that we will inherit?

3. How central to the gospel is the doctrine of justification? Is it the heart of the gospel, without which there is no good news? How do you prioritize justification among the many truths of our salvation?

Day 38

Titus 3:7b

READ

... heirs according to the hope of eternal life.

MEDITATE

We are going to extend our meditation on this verse for one additional day, as more needs to be discussed about the hope we have of eternal life. What exactly is "eternal life"? There are several things to be said about these two words. First, although it is obvious, this life we have from God is endless. It is a life that has no expiration date. It is indestructible and derives from the very life of God himself. If a born-again believer in Jesus who is given eternal life could fully and finally apostatize and forfeit their salvation, the life formerly given would not have been eternal. It would have been temporary.

We can rest confidently that this life is guaranteed because it has been promised to us by the God who cannot lie. The opening of Titus contains Paul's commitment to the elect of God, "in hope of eternal life, which God, who never lies, promised before the ages began" (Titus 1:2). The apostle John reaffirms this truth: "And this is the promise that he made to us—eternal life" (1 John

2:25). God always comes through on his promises, and the commitment he has made to us of eternal life is no exception.

Second, this life is both a present possession and a future promise. We are told repeatedly that God has already given us this life (1 John 5:11). Indeed, it is said in the present tense: "whoever has the Son *has* life" (1 John 5:12). John writes his first epistle to those who believe in the name of the Son of God "that you may know that you *have* eternal life" (again, present tense; 1 John 5:13). The fact that Paul twice says we live in hope of eternal life (Titus 1:2; 3:7) indicates that although we have it now, there is yet more to come. The consummation of the life we now have is yet future.

Third, our eternal life is both physical and spiritual. The physical dimension of this life consists in the promise that our bodies will be fully redeemed, glorified, and transformed into the likeness of the body of Christ himself (see Phil 3:20–21; Rom 8:18–25). It is in that yet glorified body that we will live forever. This life is also profoundly spiritual in that we have experienced "the washing of regeneration" by the Spirit (Titus 3:5), and we are (and forever will be) forgiven of all our sins, justified by faith in Christ, and perfectly reconciled to our great Triune God.

There is, of course, an alternative to eternal life through faith in Christ. It is eternal, irreversible death or final separation from the presence and glory of God. The Bible's most famous verse sets in contrast the possibility of eternal life or eternal death when it says, "For God so loved the world, that he gave his only Son, that whoever believes in him should not perish but have eternal life" (John 3:16). There are only two options available to us: unending life and joy and peace in the presence of God or unending death and misery and anguish in his absence (see 2 Thess 1:9).

REFLECT ON CHRIST

Our eternal life is inextricably connected to the Lord Jesus Christ. First John 5:11 unapologetically asserts that the eternal life given to us by the Father "is in his Son." Life cannot be found or known or experienced apart from the Son, in whom we have been placed and are now united by faith. This is why John can say that "whoever has the Son has life; whoever does not have the Son does not have life" (1 John 5:12). Many today who are alive physically have no part in the Son. Only those who are in the Son by faith have life that is everlasting.

Non-Christian religions contend that, because they affirm the existence of a god and instruct their followers in altruistic and sacrificial living, this is sufficient to secure eternal life. There are even some professing Christians who argue that acknowledging the existence and power and goodness of the God of Scripture is enough to receive eternal life. But Scripture is clear: one must have the Son to have life (1 John 5:12). John could not have made his point with greater clarity when he said that "no one who denies the Son has the Father. Whoever confesses the Son has the Father also" (1 John 2:23).

APPLY GOD'S WORD

Knowing that we now have eternal life and will remain alive in Christ forever is a powerful incentive for both godly living and worship. Throughout this letter, Paul has encouraged Titus, and by application, all Christians, to pursue a life of godliness (Titus 2:1–14; 3:1–2). This is especially clear in Titus 3:8–11, which follows immediately upon 3:7. In other words, it is the eternal life that we have been graciously given (v. 7) that undergirds and empowers our commitment to devote ourselves "to good works" (v. 8).

We do not pursue good works to gain life, but we do so out of love for the God who has already blessed us with it. Sadly, many live with an if/then approach to Christianity: If I do this, then God will love and accept me. Paul would contend for a because/therefore approach to Christian living. *Because* we have been loved and accepted and made recipients of eternal life, *therefore* we devote ourselves to good works. If/then thinking breeds legalism and self-righteousness. Because/therefore thinking grounds our obedience in the prior free grace and love of the God who has already done everything to secure eternal life for us in Christ.

PRAY

Great God and heavenly Father, how can I say thanks for the incredible gift of eternal life? I know that I deserve eternal death, but in your kindness and mercy you have chosen to regenerate my heart and impart life everlasting. May the reality of the present possession and future hope of eternal life energize me in my commitment to you. May the Holy Spirit awaken in me each day a fresh understanding of the majesty of this breathtaking gift of grace. Amen.

STUDY IT FURTHER

1. What is the difference between biblical hope and wishful thinking? On what is our hope based?
2. How does hope in something yet future serve to fuel obedience and sacrifice in the present? Do some people become so heaven-focused regarding future promises that they cease to be of any earthly good in the present? If yes, why? If no, why not?

3. Read Romans 5:2. What is the relationship between our hope "in the glory of God" and our hope "of eternal life"?

Day 39

Titus 3:8–11

READ

The saying is trustworthy, and I want you to insist on these things, so that those who have believed in God may be careful to devote themselves to good works. These things are excellent and profitable for people. But avoid foolish controversies, genealogies, dissensions, and quarrels about the law, for they are unprofitable and worthless. As for a person who stirs up division, after warning him once and then twice, have nothing more to do with him, knowing that such a person is warped and sinful; he is self-condemned.

MEDITATE

Paul prefaces his three primary exhortations in this paragraph with the reminder that what he is about to say is "trustworthy" (v. 8a; the same wording appears in 1 Tim 1:15; 3:1; 4:9; 2 Tim 2:11; for more, see my comments on 2 Tim 2:11). Simply put, you can count on this. It is deserving of your confidence. The "saying" itself is likely a reference both to the truths of verses 1–7 as well as the threefold charge that follows.

First, Paul wants Titus to stand firmly on these matters and speak confidently of them. This is no time for hesitancy or cowardice or soft-pedaling the truth. Those whose faith in God is genuine, over against those whose profession of faith is betrayed by their evil deeds (1:16), must demonstrate the reality of their belief by the quality of their good works (3:8).

Second, in contrast to the good works that are "excellent and profitable," there are certain issues that must be avoided. Paul doesn't want Titus (or us) to waste our time engaging in "foolish controversies." There are certain doctrines and ideas worth fighting for (such as the truths expressed in 2:11–14 and 3:4–7), and there are numerous conflicts that erupt in the body of Christ that have no substantive content or moral value (see 1:14). Debates and speculations surrounding genealogies (perhaps speculations and myths relating to the pedigree of well-known Old Testament persons), as well as arguments about minute and comparatively unimportant matters of law, are to be avoided. There are undoubtedly "excellent and profitable" (v. 8b) things to which we must devote ourselves, just as there are "unprofitable and worthless" (v. 9b) issues that we must shun.

Third, disciplinary steps are to be taken against any "person who stirs up division" (v. 10). This phrase is the translation of a single word in Greek, from which we have derived our term "heretic." The focus here is on the way in which such people divide the body of Christ through those useless quarrels mentioned in verse 9. Paul's concept of a heretic, then, is a person who promotes false teaching in such a way that it undermines unity and creates factions in the body of Christ. Put in contemporary terms, a heretic is a hard-headed, contentious loudmouth whose stubbornness and arrogance cause trouble.

Paul gives clear instruction on how such a person is to be handled. They should be given two warnings, which indicates that the aim of discipline is restoration. But why only two warnings? The likelihood is that if such a person has not repented by then, they never will. To prolong the process only gives them unwarranted and unprofitable publicity.

If the counsel in verse 10 seems severe, Paul reminds us that such a person is "warped and sinful" (v. 11a). Literally, they have become perverted and are sinning. The refusal to heed the warning and remain unrepentant is evidence of a twisted mind and morally deficient character. By their actions they have brought justified condemnation upon themselves. Therefore, have nothing more to do with them.

REFLECT ON CHRIST

The Father's love for the church is clearly seen in Acts 20:28 where Paul urges elders "to care for the church of God, which he obtained with his own blood." The latter phrase should probably be translated, "with the blood of his own," in other words, with that of his own Son, Jesus. The Son also loves the church: "Christ loved the church and gave himself up for her" (Eph 5:25). Our love for the church (notwithstanding its obvious and inexcusable flaws) must be like that which Christ himself displayed when he gave his life up on the cross to redeem her.

The reason for this reminder is that church discipline is inextricably tied to Christology. Firm steps against those who disrupt and divide the local church are justified because of our commitment to the honor of Christ Jesus. The purity and public testimony of the body of Christ reflects directly on its Lord and Savior. This helps explain why Paul took such a strong stand with the church in Corinth. He was shocked that they had permitted the sort of sexual immorality "that is not tolerated even among pagans" (1 Cor 5:1). If the name of Christ is to be upheld, firm (but loving) discipline must be enacted against those whose behavior brings reproach on the gospel.

APPLY GOD'S WORD

Church discipline is a sadly neglected, often altogether ignored, biblical obligation. It isn't that church leaders should go searching out every manner of error, but they must be prepared to take steps to deal with the sort of unrepentant immoral behavior and theological deviations that dishonor the person and work of Christ.

The purposes of church discipline are many: to maintain, as far as possible, the purity of the church (1 Cor 3:17), to provide a Christ-exalting witness to the world, to facilitate growth and preserve the unity of the body (Eph 4:1–16), to expose unbelievers (1 John 2:19), to restore the erring brother or sister to obedience and fellowship (1 Cor 5:5; 2 Cor 2:6–10; Gal 6:1; 2 Thess 3:14–15), to deter others (1 Tim 5:20), and to avert corporate discipline from the Lord (Rev 2:14–25). It would also appear that Paul believed the willingness to embrace the task of discipline was a mark of maturity in a church's corporate life (2 Cor 2:9).

Few things are as painful and distressing as dealing with a professing believer who refuses to heed the call to repentance. But it is absolutely necessary not only for the honor of Christ's name in the community but for the temporal and eternal welfare of the wayward believer.

PRAY

Father, forgive me for following after useless and ultimately divisive doctrines. I confess that I am prone to major on minors and thereby produce divisions over issues that simply don't matter all that much. Keep my eyes set on the fundamental truths of your word. Keep my heart fixed on the foundational principles of both good theology and good works. May I, in all that I believe, honor and extol the name of my great Savior, Jesus Christ. Amen.

STUDY IT FURTHER

1. Paul clearly believed that there was a direct cause-and-effect relationship between the insistence on the truth of the gospel and the commitment of the Christian to good works. What precisely is that relationship? Why is the former so essential for the latter?

2. "Foolish controversies" were obviously a problem in the first century. What are some of these still operative in our day? Have you been involved in quarrels about such matters? If so, what profit did they have? How should they be avoided in the future?

3. Is it consistent for Paul to speak of certain people as "warped and sinful" without violating his earlier command that we "speak evil of no one"? How do you reconcile these two statements?

Day 40

Titus 3:12–15

READ

When I send Artemas or Tychicus to you, do your best to come to me at Nicopolis, for I have decided to spend the winter there. Do your best to speed Zenas the lawyer and Apollos on their way; see that they lack nothing. And let our people learn to devote themselves to good works, so as to help cases of urgent need, and not be unfruitful. All who are with me send greetings to you. Greet those who love us in the faith. Grace be with you all.

MEDITATE

Whenever we come across a passage in the Bible like Titus 3:12–15, we must think about what Paul said in 2 Timothy 3:16–17: "All Scripture is breathed out by God and profitable for teaching, for reproof, for correction, and for training in righteousness, that the man of God may be complete, equipped for every good work."

Sometimes we fail to emphasize the first word in that text: *all.* Did Paul really mean that, or did he only have in mind the more important, more theological, more foundational statements in Scripture? I can certainly understand how this verse speaks to the importance of Titus 1:5–9, as well as 2:11–14 and 3:4–7. But are the concluding salutations and personal instructions in a text like Titus 3:12–15 included in the "all" that Paul declares was breathed out by God and serves to build us up in our faith? Yes. It is. If nothing else, it demonstrates to us the concern Paul had for people who otherwise might not seem to matter. It is an example of the vital roles that all God's people can play in the work of ministry.

Artemas is only mentioned in this one text in the New Testament. Tychicus is described by Paul as "the beloved brother and faithful minister" and "fellow servant in the Lord" (Eph 6:21 and Col 4:7; see also Acts 20:4 and 2 Tim 4:12). He may well have been the carrier of the letters to the Ephesians and Colossians, and the second letter to Timothy. Needless to say, he was highly trustworthy and of preeminent value to Paul. Zenas, a lawyer, and Apollos were probably the two men who carried this letter to Titus.

Paul apparently cannot let the opportunity pass to mention once again the importance of God's people devoting themselves to "good works" (see also 2:7, 14; 3:1, 8). Of the many good works that might have been mentioned, Paul focuses on helping those in the church who have urgent needs, most likely financial in nature.

Another important matter we overlook when we neglect passages like this is the exhortation to greet one another. In Romans 16:1–6, Paul exhorts them to greet this or that person no fewer than thirteen times. Paul undoubtedly meant more than that they should say, "Paul says hello." Or, "Greetings from the apostle." I suspect that the leaders in the churches at Rome and on the island of Crete would seek out the people whom the apostle mentions and say something along the lines of: "You'll never believe this, but the apostle Paul has been thinking about you and praying for you. He specifically told us to let you know that he loves you and hopes to see you soon. You mean a lot to him and the distance by which you are separated does not in the least diminish his heartfelt affection for you." The encouragement Paul gives to the people around him should not be overlooked. Like Paul, we should be seeking out opportunities to strengthen and encourage those around us with a heartfelt greeting.

REFLECT ON CHRIST

As we bring our time in Titus to an end, we should pay close attention to Paul's final words: "Grace be with you all" (v. 15b). Although the letter is addressed personally to Titus (1:4), Paul includes everyone on the island of Crete "who love us in the faith." What should we make of the apostle's desire that God's grace be with them?

Perhaps the answer to this question is found in Paul's own experience of God's grace as described in 2 Corinthians 12. This chapter contains the account of Paul's translation into the third heaven where "he heard things that cannot be told, which man may not utter" (2 Cor 12:4). "So," writes Paul, "to keep me from becoming conceited because of the surpassing greatness of the revelations, a thorn was given me in the flesh … to keep me from becoming conceited" (2 Cor 12:7). When Paul finally realized that Jesus would not remove the annoying thorn, he heard Jesus say, "My grace is sufficient for you, for my power is made perfect in weakness" (2 Cor 12:9). This grace upheld and sustained Paul, empowering him to endure the pain. This, I believe, is the same sort of grace or power of God's presence that the apostle now prays would be imparted to Titus. And this grace likewise will do the same for you and me, whatever trying circumstances we may encounter.

APPLY GOD'S WORD

How often do you pray for God's grace to fill your heart, soul, mind, and body? When you find yourself weak and suffering, or even when faced with a challenge that stretches your talents beyond what you can endure in your own strength, do you cry out for the same manifestation of grace that Paul prayed for on behalf of Titus and the others in Crete?

As we've noticed before, grace is more than the aspect of God's character by which he saved us. After all, Paul has earlier mentioned that we have been "justified by his grace" (v. 7). Indeed, the entirety of our salvation is traceable to God's grace, over against the tendency we all feel to rely upon our own good works (Eph 2:8–9). But grace is also power. When Paul felt utterly burdened by his thorn in the flesh, Jesus did not tell him to meditate or reflect on the gratuitous nature of his salvation. Instead, he assured the apostle that his grace was sufficient for him. By this Jesus meant that the indwelling presence of the Holy Spirit would energize his weary soul and hurting body to persevere. The thorn will remain, Jesus said, but so too will the strength of divine grace to enable you to endure. It is no less true for us today than it was for Paul and Titus then.

PRAY

Father, I am a weak and needy person. My body grows weary from disease. My soul is increasingly vexed and frustrated by the sin in and around me. I find myself lacking wisdom to navigate the many challenges and decisions of life in this fallen and corrupt world. I cry out to you now that by the power of your grace you would strengthen me in my weakness, that you would enlighten my eyes to understand, and that you would equip me in every way to persevere in good works and humble confidence in Christ, all for his great glory. Amen.

STUDY IT FURTHER

1. Can you identify specific instances when the grace of God was noticeably with you to empower, sustain, and encourage you in the face of the many problems this world poses? Specifically, how did you sense God's grace working in and through you?

2. Paul speaks of "those who love us in the faith." To what does the word "faith" refer? Does Paul mean we are only responsible to love those who agree with us on all Christian doctrine? If not, how might you go about obeying his directive?

3. Why does one's faith matter when it comes to loving others? And how does this love differ from the love we are responsible to show those who are outside of the Christian faith?

Group Reading Plan

What follows is a suggested plan for reading through this study in a group, with six days of study per week.

WEEK 1

1. Introduction to 2 Timothy and Titus
2. 2 Timothy 1:1–2
3. 2 Timothy 1:3
4. 2 Timothy 1:4–5
5. 2 Timothy 1:6–7
6. 2 Timothy 1:8

WEEK 2

1. 2 Timothy 1:9–12a
2. 2 Timothy 1:12b
3. 2 Timothy 1:13–14
4. 2 Timothy 1:15–18
5. 2 Timothy 2:1–2
6. 2 Timothy 2:3–6

WEEK 3

1. 2 Timothy 2:7
2. 2 Timothy 2:8
3. 2 Timothy 2:9
4. 2 Timothy 2:10
5. 2 Timothy 2:11–13
6. 2 Timothy 2:14–19

WEEK 4

1. 2 Timothy 2:20–21
2. 2 Timothy 2:22–26
3. 2 Timothy 3:1–9
4. 2 Timothy 3:10–13
5. 2 Timothy 3:14–17
6. 2 Timothy 4:1–5

WEEK 5

1. 2 Timothy 4:6–8
2. 2 Timothy 4:9–15
3. 2 Timothy 4:16–18
4. 2 Timothy 4:19–22
5. Titus 1:1–4
6. Titus 1:5–9

WEEK 6

1. Titus 1:10–16
2. Titus 2:1–6
3. Titus 2:7–10
4. Titus 2:11–12
5. Titus 2:13–15
6. Titus 3:1–3

WEEK 7

1. Titus 3:4–5
2. Titus 3:6–7
3. Titus 3:7b
4. Titus 3:8–11
5. Titus 3:12–15